MIND & MEDICINE MONOGRAPHS

Editor

MICHAEL BALINT, M.D., PH.D., M.SC.

7

*The Caseworker's
Use of
Relationships*

MIND & MEDICINE MONOGRAPHS

EDITORIAL ADVISORY BOARD

The Caseworker's Use of Relationships

MARGARET L. FERARD

AND

NOËL K. HUNNYBUN

Foreword by
JOHN BOWLBY
M.A., M.D.

TAVISTOCK PUBLICATIONS

CHARLES C THOMAS · PUBLISHER

First published in 1962
by Tavistock Publications (1959) Limited
11 New Fetter Lane, London E.C.4
and printed in Great Britain
in 11 point Times Roman by
C. Tinling & Co. Ltd., Liverpool, London, and Prescot

★

First published in 1962
in the United States of America
by Charles C Thomas · Publisher
301-327 East Lawrence Avenue, Springfield, Illinois

CONTENTS

FOREWORD

"There's now't as queer as folk" is an old saying and an inconveniently true one. Were everyone to behave with reason and to order his life with sweet commonsense, to help him would be easy—though perhaps unnecessary. As it is, our actions are often far from sensible and we find ourselves our own worst enemies. Good advice we ignore, and only advice that suits our preconceived plans do we accept. That makes the job of helping us and others peculiarly difficult. Sooner or later everyone who sets out on a career of medical or social service will find that human nature is very awkward stuff with which to work. This means that, like the artist, if he is to achieve results, he must study his medium.

The two authors of this book are British caseworkers who began their careers when economic distress was prevalent and the obvious needs of material welfare masked the unpalatable fact that, as the religious tradition has always known, man is beset also by ills other than those of poverty. The authors in their professional work discovered that jealousy, suspicion, anxiety, grief, anger, longing, and many another feeling of great intensity can also blight a person's life; and that, moreover, the troubles that arise from feelings are often far more difficult to mend than those that arise from lack of means. They had to learn a new way to look at people and new ways of providing help. For them the application of

vii

psycho-analytic principles to their work has been a simple practical necessity.

The usual way in which psycho-analysis is presented is in terms of libidinal phases, id, ego, and super-ego, and others of the ambitious yet tentative theories that from time to time Freud advanced in the hope of providing a conceptual framework for his observations. All too often, indeed, these theories are presented as though the core of psycho-analysis is in some way enshrined in them. Nothing is further from the truth. "Such ideas as these", Freud remarks, "are part of a speculative superstructure of psycho-analysis, any portion of which can be abandoned or changed without loss or regret the moment its inadequacy has been proved." The foundations are far more solid: they are our observations of how people behave and talk in their daily lives, and especially the unexpected ways in which they tend to treat us when they seek our help.

It is therefore refreshing to find the authors of this book introducing the reader to the foundations of psycho-analysis instead of to its speculative superstructure. Here is a succession of sketches of human beings in distress presented to illustrate the way in which each views the situation in which he finds himself through a private pair of spectacles, and some of the ways in which unknowingly each has come by his particular pair. This is where Freud started and where every student is wise to begin. The first task of the would-be helper is to understand the nature of the problem that is besetting her client. Since this problem is as often as not a product of distorted perceptions and inept behaviour derived from them, the worker must learn to know what the world looks like through spectacles other than her own. Only then will she find her client's feelings and behaviour intelligible and be able to find a common ground on which to meet. Only then will she realize that reassurance is usually foolish and that the course of action that at first sight seems so obvious a solution is one that her client either could not contemplate or else could not execute with success.

In recent years caseworkers have sometimes been told that their job is to meet their clients' overt requests and not to seek for other and unspoken ones. In a doctor's ears such advice rings strangely. It is as though he were told that his job was to treat the symptoms of which his patient complains and to avoid making an examination to discover whence they derive. Following the medical pattern, the authors describe some of the ways in which a casework investigation can be made and some of the findings that it commonly reveals. They also emphasize that, while a proper investigation and diagnosis are essential if inappropriate measures are to be avoided, in going further it is imperative "to refrain from exceeding the client's mandate". The caseworker's recognition that the major problem is different from the overt one resembles the doctor's in conferring on her no right of intervention. It is for the client, like the patient, to decide whether or not he wishes the problem which has been revealed to be dealt with.

Perhaps no aspect of psycho-analytic thought has given rise to so much misunderstanding and misplaced caution as transference. Sometimes it has been thought that caseworkers should avoid arousing transference reactions, as though there was some magic that could put a stop to them. Others have thought that, although they were bound to occur and should therefore be understood, reference to them was dangerous. Finally, there have been those who have believed it to be legitimate to refer to manifestations of positive transference but not to those of negative. Fifteen years of teaching and supervising casework students at the Tavistock Clinic, for seven of which Miss Hunnybun was senior tutor, have convinced me that such ideas would be as absurd in practice as they undoubtedly are in theory. Transference reactions and counter-transference reactions are the stuff of which the case-worker's daily life is made. Her job is not to avoid them but to learn how best to deal with them, recognizing always that the way the client and she treat each other is neither wholly a mere repetition of their past nor wholly a matter-of-fact coping with the present, but the result by each of an un-conscious appraisal of the present in terms of more or less similar situations that each has experienced in the past. How could it ever be otherwise?

How and when usefully to interpret transference reactions can hardly be taught in a book. But an orientation can be taught. Above all, the beginner needs to be able to distinguish clearly between his own perceptions of what is occurring and questions of when and how he may be able to communicate his knowledge fruitfully. As the authors so rightly emphasize, wisdom and discretion in choosing the moment are the crux of the matter. These can be learned only in the course of experience, guided by supervision from those with more experience than oneself.

The authors are among the first British caseworkers to have recognized the value of systematic supervision, to have learnt how it is best done, and to have taught it to others. Their contribution to the development of British casework is already great. By presenting their experience in this lucid and vivid form they will put a much larger public in their debt. For they have written a book which provides an admirable introduction for anyone—whether in casework, nursing, or medicine, and whether qualified or still a student—who wishes to know how to understand human beings in order better to help them.

JOHN BOWLBY

AUTHORS' PREFACE

This book is the result of many years of practice in the social-casework field. In it we have discussed certain psycho-analytical concepts which we have found of value in our work. This has been a difficult task, and we realize that often we have failed to do justice to our subject. Nevertheless, we hope that what we have attempted may contribute to casework thinking and practice.

Our thanks are due to colleagues, students, and clients who have made the writing of this book a possibility. Our special acknowledgments are extended to Irmi Elkan, Matilda Goldberg, and Elizabeth Irvine for their generous help and advice during its compilation and to Madge Dongray and Arthur Hunt for some of the case material offered in Part II. We should also like to thank those who have patiently carried out the typing of the manuscript.

MARGARET L. FERARD
NOËL K. HUNNYBUN

PART I

CHAPTER 1

An Approach to
the Understanding of People. I

It is in the nature of casework that those who engage in it are brought into touch with all sorts and conditions of men, because people differ so greatly from each other and each client comes to the agency with his[1] own particular outlook on life and with his own particular feelings and attitudes about the problems and difficulties with which he is seeking help. At the one extreme is the client who in the main is self-determining and self-reliant and therefore able, as a rule, to face the ups and downs of life realistically and carry his responsibilities adequately: he is unlikely to come to the agency unless overtaken by fortuitous disaster and is probably well able to judge for himself whether the services placed at his disposal are likely to meet his need and to make good use of them should they appeal to him. At the other extreme is the client who is a somewhat childlike person who has to depend on others for help in time of need: he is probably a frequent visitor to the agency because he finds it difficult or impossible to cope with life unaided and it may

[1] It will be convenient in the text to refer to the caseworker as "she" and to the client as "he".

3

be that he is his own worst enemy in that, for reasons deeply buried in his mind, he tends to behave in ways that serve to promote and perpetuate his misfortunes and that nullify attempts made by others to help him. For instance, should he ask for help with a practical problem, he perhaps finds sundry reasons that seem to him to render unsuitable such reasonable suggestions as are made to him as to how it might be eased or overcome; nevertheless he returns for further advice, only to act once more in the same way. Or it may be that he immediately turns such suggestions aside in favour of his own plans from which he is not to be deterred although from the standpoint of common sense they have little chance of succeeding.

The fact that no two individuals respond in exactly the same way to help offered in time of need, even although their respective problems may seem to have much in common, is borne out in every casework setting and is an indication of how widely people differ from each other in their capacity to believe in their own helpability as well as in the degree to which they are able to credit the possible goodness of others towards them. These differences in people explain why case-work can never be a matter of routine and why, in seeking ways of helping, it is necessary to have a sensitive awareness in each instance of the kind of person the client is—that is to say, whether he is relatively realistic in his outlook on life and in his ways of feeling, thinking, and acting, or the reverse, and how he is prone to feel towards himself and his problem and towards others in relation to himself. When this natural sensitivity to people as individuals is present and when there is a real desire on the part of the caseworker to try to appreciate the client's problem and difficulties from his point of view, consideration of some of the dis-coveries of psycho-analysis can be immensely helpful because of the understanding of people which they make possible. For

4

instance, it is now known that behaviour often cannot be fully explained solely in terms of common sense, because psychoanalysis has shown that the individual is all the time and in varying degrees being prompted in what he says and does by deeply buried parts of the mind, which do not function in commonsense ways. In other words, he is being influenced by the unconscious, which has a rich and varied life of its own and is subject to special laws which are very different to those of conscious thought.

This is a vast subject, which obviously can only be touched on in a book such as this, but it is essential to point out that the unconscious is really completely unconscious, although it is all the time actively at work in each person, influencing his day-to-day life in various ways and in varying degrees. This helps to explain why no one can be entirely practical in outlook or behave unfailingly in ways that are in keeping with common sense, and why even those who are highly gifted in many respects may tend to lack sound judgment in ordinary matters and find it difficult or impossible to modify their behaviour or change it solely by an effort of will. It is also necessary to point out that there is a tendency on the part of the unconscious to strive to enter consciousness, and that in so far as it succeeds in doing so it loses its compelling force and ceases to influence feeling, thought, and action. Although it is not the function of the caseworker to attempt to explore the depths of the mind even should she be competent to do so, it is her function to be familiar with the common ways in which the unconscious tends to manifest itself in peoples' lives, because in this way she will be able to recognize the nature of the client's problems and difficulties more fully than would otherwise be possible, and hence to recognize as well the kind of help that is needed. And it is perhaps a useful thought to bear in mind that should his behaviour appear odd or unaccountable and to lack explanation at first sight, it

B

would probably be found to have meaning were it possible to look with knowledge and understanding into the parts of his mind that are not normally accessible either to himself or others. This kind of awareness opens up channels of communication between worker and client that might otherwise remain closed, and paves the way to the sensitive use of such common casework methods as discussion, advice about practical difficulties, the giving of material help, and the consideration of conscious emotional problems that are proving a hindrance to social adjustment. These matters will be considered later in relation to actual casework practice, and after drawing attention to three cases that illustrate some of the points made.

The first case is that of a married woman with four children who applies to a social agency for financial aid at a time when the family income is less than usual owing to her husband's ill health and unemployment. Having made her application, she immediately and protestingly says that she is not willing to accept help from the worker or anyone else, because she knows from experience that "they never help you properly in these places"; she goes on to say that she doubts whether her confidence will be respected, and emphasizes with reason that she can ill spare the time which is being incurred in coming to the agency although she is apparently eager to talk at length. She tells the worker spontaneously and with some indignation that when she was a child she had been obliged to look after her small brothers and sisters and to do the housework early in the morning before going to school, because it was necessary for her widowed mother to go out to work in order to eke out the family income. She explains that her mother never recognized her need "to play about like other children" and had made her "run before I could stand on my feet"

6

—in fact the childhood picture she has retained of herself is that of a little girl who is always unloved and exploited. She then tells the worker about the children and says that, whereas formerly her husband had been able to maintain the family in moderate comfort, he has not been able to do so recently on account of ill health and unemployment and that, because of these misfortunes, she has lately been obliged to forgo many small comforts on which she had come to rely. As she unfolds her story it becomes apparent that she is deeply resentful towards the husband, whom she considers has "let me down", and that in her heart of hearts she is unwilling to try to cope with practical difficulties, feeling that it is his responsibility to do so—not hers. She refers indignantly to social agencies where she has already applied for help, at the same time emphasizing that she "does not want charity". She tells the worker with some vehemence that she has a trade she could follow at home if she wished, but that she sees no reason why she should do so since it is clearly the job of others to come to her rescue especially as she has four young children dependent on her. She again says with feeling that she would "rather starve" than accept charity, apparently seeing no discrepancy between this remark and the fact that she is now approaching yet another agency.

Although the client's refusal to accept financial help is obviously against her interest and therefore unreasonable, the meaning of her behaviour begins to become clear when some of the unconscious feelings and attitudes that underlie and prompt it are glimpsed. What seems to be happening is perhaps roughly as follows. When she comes to the agency apparently both wanting help and at the same time not wanting it, it can be inferred that she is at the mercy of feelings that have been rankling for a long time, which, stemming

7

from her unhappy childhood when she probably felt she did not get good things because she did not deserve them, cause her to feel that she is now expected to carry the whole burden of the home and that no one sympathizes with her or appreciates her. She does not want to carry out the tasks with which she is confronted because she unconsciously carries over from situations of the past on to the current situation the attitude "I am an unloved child on whom everyone places undue burdens; this I must prove to the world and therefore it is impossible for me to accept help, much as I want it"; hence her attitude to the worker, whom she partly sees as the unloving mother of long ago, and hence, too, her attitude to her husband and the young children who so forcibly remind her of the irksome burdens of the past.

Thus, for reasons that are unconscious, she is unable either to believe that the worker can want to help her or to accept the financial assistance she might receive, which would make it possible for her to come to the aid of her family. In her own words she would "rather starve", though like a peevish and difficult child she continues to seek help, while at the same time refusing it. And perhaps, deeply buried in her unconscious mind, is the wish that someone shall try to help her to understand the feelings which, stemming from her childhood, are now so greatly inhibiting her actions and at the same time hindering her from carrying her adult responsibilities. But of this she would of course be quite unaware. And perhaps guilt about her hostility towards her mother in the old days is impelling her to self-punishment and is thus standing between herself and the help she is needing. Of course it may well be that from time to time she has had reason for being critical of agencies and workers, since no agency is without fault and the best of workers cannot be unfailingly sympathetic and tactful. But her outlook on life is such that she has probably always found people unhelpful, however willing they may have been to assist her; it may also well be that, in view of the difficult circumstances of her early days she has reason enough to think ill of her mother, but in any case this is how she regards her, whatever the realities may have been.

The following case also shows that much light can be thrown on a client's present difficulties by seeing them in relation to past experiences. An elderly woman, neatly dressed in black, comes of her own accord to consult a worker. She appears very tense and worried and as if on the verge of tears, her black clothes and sad expression leading the worker to wonder whether she has perhaps suffered a recent bereavement. She immediately says that she is very worried about her future because she has decided that she must give up her job although she fears that because of her advancing age another may not easily come her way. She goes on to describe her apprehension of becoming homeless and poverty-stricken and says that she has come to ask the worker's advice as to what she should do—should she give up her job or should she keep it? However, she does not appear to be particularly interested in what the worker might advise, but continues to talk of her troubles. She says that for the last few months she has held a resident domestic post as housekeeper to a middle-aged couple, in whose service she has come to feel unable to remain because she believes they have taken a dislike to her and are impossible people to please. She describes her life with them as sheer misery, in that everything she does seems to be wrong and she is exploited and under-valued. She goes on to explain, however, that in many ways her post has certain advantages—for instance, she has good wages and many material comforts which she is reluctant to forgo.

9

Unlike the last client described, she volunteered little information about her childhood beyond the fact that it was spent at home with her parents and a brother several years her senior and that they were a closely knit family. It emerges that her parents died at an advanced age when she was in the late forties, and that during their last years she had bestowed much care upon them and had made every effort to be a good daughter and home-maker. But at times she had found them critical, exacting, and hard to please, so that she had suffered a painful sense of frustration and injustice. During the interview with the worker the client stresses the love she had felt for the old parents and the home but acknowledges that there were many occasions when she found her "job" a somewhat thankless one because they did not seem to realize how hard she worked and "took her for granted". She goes on to say that after they died she and her brother continued to live in the old home and that she had acted as housekeeper for him as he had remained a bachelor and had needed someone to look after him. This arrangement had suited them well because his earnings together with her own small income had enabled them to live in reasonable comfort without undue anxiety as to ways and means. But to her great dismay her brother had married and brought his wife to the home, and as she tells her story it becomes clear that from this time onwards she has tended to see him as unkind and rejecting whereas previously she had found him benevolent and protecting. Therefore, there is a sense in which she has undoubtedly suffered a very real bereavement, which is perhaps made more poignant by the fact that she now finds herself with a rival in the person of her sister-in-law who, together with the brother, seems to her to have ousted her from her place in the home she has known all her life and where she no longer seems to have a niche. After a period of painful indecision as to whether she should fall in with the suggestion

10

of her brother and sister-in-law that she should remain a member of the household, or whether she would do better to live elsewhere, she decided on the latter course and obtained the resident domestic post as a way of solving her predicament.

For the purposes of the present discussion it is of note that, having taken this step, the client experiences feelings and attitudes in her relationship with her employers that clearly bear comparison with those she had already experienced in her relationship with her brother and sister-in-law. Once more it seems to her that she has no place in the "home" and that those in her immediate circle are unsympathetic towards her, and once more she finds herself in a state of painful indecision as to what to do for the best. Obviously the possibility cannot be ruled out that the elderly couple by whom she is now employed are in fact somewhat lacking in consideration for her and that they do not appreciate her services, but there can be little doubt that past emotional experiences with people predispose her to regard her employers as at fault and herself as the injured party. Perhaps, therefore, she seeks out the worker less for the conscious reason of asking advice as to whether she should remain in her job or leave it and more because, either consciously or unconsciously, she is wanting help with the welter of feelings which become re-evoked in her in her new "home" and which surround the job she is finding so uncongenial but which she does not entirely want to relinquish. It is of note that the parents for whom she had cared in the past did not always seem to her to appreciate the services she rendered them.

The third case illustrates that sometimes an emotional problem may be less keenly felt than its seriousness justifies when it is accompanied by one of a different kind, in this

11

instance an environmental one. An anxious and distressed woman comes to the agency for help with a housing problem on the grounds that her flat is in such poor condition that she feels it is injuring the health of herself and her children. A home visit reveals that the family is living in old, damp, and dilapidated property which has little chance of being repaired and that her request is therefore not only entirely reasonable but one that requires to be met with as little delay as possible. It is of interest that, although the client is obviously very worried and unhappy about her bad housing and longs to move to better surroundings, a serious marital problem which becomes revealed in the course of her talks with the worker does not seem to be causing her so much concern. Perhaps what is happening is that she is unconsciously shifting or displacing on to the bad housing many feelings concerning her unhappy marriage, which in consequence is not causing her the degree of distress that might have been expected, the environmental problem thus having the ironic advantage of helping to keep her unaware of the deeper cause of her unhappiness. If this is so, it might be anticipated that, even were she to find herself and her family suitably rehoused, she would not feel satisfied because she would continue to be unconsciously impelled to displace her feelings elsewhere for so long as her marital problem persists. And it should perhaps be pointed out that, while the worker would of course do her best to help the client to find other and better accommodation as soon as possible she would also hope to afford her opportunity for receiving help with her marital problem.

The cases described above raise questions that are closely bound up with casework. For instance, why is one person more able than another to accept help that would seem both

12

suitable and timely and in accordance with his apparent need? Again, how can inklings be gained from time to time of the unconscious feelings and thoughts that are prompting a client to ask for advice yet be unwilling to accept it even though it would seem pertinent to the situation he has described? Although such questions cannot be answered precisely, because many factors combine in causing each individual to become the kind of person he now is and to meet life in his own particular fashion, psycho-analysis has demonstrated that the relationships an individual establishes with those who had the care of him in his early days are among the most important influences that have shaped his life, because they are the pattern or prototype of all subsequent relationships. This is why this subject of early relationships and their importance for later life merits the thought and attention of caseworkers who want to deepen their understanding of individual clients; it throws light not only on the nature of the relationships he has established with his family and circle, but also on the nature of his present relationship with the worker who is seeking to help him with his various problems and difficulties.

Attention will be drawn in the next chapter to some of the findings of psycho-analysis that would seem to have particular relevance for work with clients, but it will need to be borne in mind throughout the whole of the discussion following that, if the discoveries of psycho-analysis concerning the ways in which people grow and develop emotionally are to have real meaning for the worker, they must be assimilated both intellectually and emotionally. Only when this is the case can they be useful aids to casework.

CHAPTER 2

An Approach to
the Understanding of People. II

Ever since the pioneer work of Freud and his followers at
the beginning of this century there has been a growing body
of formulated knowledge about the nature and range of the
feelings that become evoked in the earliest relationships of
life, and in this way much light has been thrown on the
significance that the individual's first experiences with people
hold for his future. The purpose of this chapter is to consider
these matters in a somewhat general way so that at a later
stage their relevance for casework may become apparent.
This will be a particularly difficult task because it will mean
trying to convey an idea of child-like ways of feeling, and
when this is attempted a quality of sophistication intrudes,
which is quite inappropriate because it belongs to ways of
thinking, and the young child is incapable of conceptual
thought, although he has strong and varied feelings. It has
been said that "the more we write and print—talking is hardly
so lethal—the more words do we reduce to weaklings and even
to corpses. What happens is that words which are supposed to
be specially picturesque or exciting appear so often that they

are taken for granted. The image behind them ceases to be effective: they dwindle . . ."[1] and it is with full awareness of these truths that this chapter is written and should be read.

It is perhaps best to take as a starting-point the fact that, at first, the child is completely dependent on his mother or on someone who stands in an equivalent relationship, for the satisfaction of all his physical and emotional needs, so that he would probably die if, for more than a short time, she were not there to look after him. Therefore in a very real way he and she together are his entire world, which to begin with is the only one he knows. This may sound obvious and simple, but it is now known that the first relationship of life is not only exclusive but also very complex, giving rise to profound emotional experiences of lasting effect. For instance, it is clearly impossible for the young child always to feel contented, however good a mother he may have, for whereas at times she satisfies his demands because he feels she gives him what he wants, there are occasions when she denies them, with the result that he feels he does *not* get what he wants. In other words, she causes him to have feelings that are good and satisfying as well as those that are bad and unsatisfying. Thus he experiences irreconcilable feelings in the first relationship of his life, and this is true whether he is breast or bottle fed. Moreover, because he naturally strives his utmost to get and keep what he wants so that he may feel satisfied and comfortable all the time, he tends to meet maternal attitudes with all the forces at his command—with feelings sometimes of love and sometimes of hate, according to whether he gets what he wants immediately or does not get it. Psycho-analysis has coined the word "ambivalent" to describe feelings that cannot be brought into accord with one another. This word is now widely current in casework circles and is correctly

[1] BROWN, IVOR. *A Word in your Ear*. London: Cape, 1942.

used when feelings are obviously mixed. Perhaps, however, it is not always realized that ambivalence in later life stems from irreconcilable feelings of love and hate experienced in infancy and revived in later relationships. This is a fact about which more will be said later, the point of interest for the moment being that ambivalent feelings and attitudes are often puzzling, but sometimes become comprehensible when they are recognized to be residues of the past as well as reactions to the immediate present.

Let us turn for the moment to consider certain maternal attitudes and the fact that the child is influenced in various ways by the nature of the care his mother gives him and the manner in which she bestows it. For instance, a tendency to respond to his forceful demands with impatience and exasperation, is likely to produce a relationship that does not afford him the satisfying feelings he craves; nevertheless, he will continue to seek them by every means at his disposal, with the result that emotional growth and development is hindered by his inability to relinquish his quest and he remains too much of a baby for too long. But if he is fortunate in having a good mother, with whom he experiences a comfortable and warm relationship because he discovers that in the main his wants are supplied, he will be able to move forward emotionally, not being prevented from doing so by a constant striving for satisfying feelings that are unattainable. In other words, he is able to begin to grow up. The importance of maternal attitudes hardly needs further emphasis except to mention, for instance, that the person who finds it hard to tolerate frustration and who tends to doubt that others may be well-disposed towards him has probably been the child who always felt thwarted, whereas the individual who is able to take the rough with the smooth and is ready to meet others half-way has probably been the child who in the main has felt secure and contented.

16

It has already been said that while he is still very young the child's world is made up of himself and his mother together. Therefore at this stage of his development he does not realize that he and she are in any way separate and different, so that, whatever may be the strength of the feelings he experiences in his relationship with her, they are not directed towards her as though she were another person but instead are experienced essentially as states of "being". It is as though he and his mother are as it were a kind of "one-ness", which he finds to be either wholly good or wholly bad, according to whether his feelings of the moment are loving because he feels his needs are being met, or unloving because he feels they are not being met. It seems, however, that when he is a few months old he begins to become aware that he and his mother are somehow different and separate, and that he gradually discovers himself as a whole person and his mother as another whole person. And so in the course of time he comes to recognize her as apart from himself, although there are reasons for supposing that he does not form a very clear idea of the kind of person she actually is.

Psycho-analysis has shown that, whether the child is breast or bottle fed, his growing awareness of himself and his mother as different beings is made possible through the experience of suckling and all that this means to him in terms of deep emotional satisfaction and the reverse. This can perhaps be appreciated when it is borne in mind that at this stage of his development his mother is to all intents and purposes the only person whose presence or absence really matters to him, and that because suckling means that sometimes she is there and that at other times she is not there, it is bound to give rise to satisfying feelings and a sense of well-being on the one hand and to unsatisfying feelings and a sense of loss on the other hand. And it seems that, as he comes to recognize her as a separate person, he discovers

17

that his own good feelings are likely to be reciprocated, and therefore he wants to please her, although sometimes he is prevented from doing so because his own forceful and primitive impulses overwhelm him, with the result that he feels a bad child, however loving and tolerant a mother he may have.

It is perhaps a manifestation of the distressing plight in which the child sometimes finds himself because of the strength of feelings that threaten to overwhelm him that he tries as it were to get rid of them. What seems to happen is that he now unconsciously attributes them to his mother, so that it appears to him that he no longer possesses them; it is as though he were removing them from where they belong and placing them on her—in other words he projects them on to her. The result is that he does not see her as entirely true to life, for when he projects feelings of hate on to her he immediately sees her as a hostile mother, whether she is actually so or not, and when he projects loving feelings on to her he immediately sees her a a loving mother, although she may not be particularly so in real life. But this is not the whole story, because simultaneously he is unconsciously taking into himself through his senses the kind of mother he sees from time to time. This is another way of saying that he introjects his own ideas of her, and that because these are not entirely correct he is continually forming mental images of her, which are in some degree fanciful. And, should it happen that feelings of goodness preponderate over feelings of badness in his projections and introjections, these images will tend to be good and benevolent, with the result that the idea of a loving mother gradually takes shape inside his mind, whereas if the opposite is the case the idea of an unloving or even hostile mother emerges. And so initially his expectations of his actual mother are more or less unrealistic; she is mixed up with his fancies, and he is prepared to find her as he

18

imagines her to be. Experience soon shows him, however, that she is not entirely as he had thought, and perhaps that she is a very different person—for instance one who is not invariably loving or invariably unloving, as previously he had believed. And so as a rule, and in course of time, he begins to test out the inner and partly fantastic mother against the real mother outside him, in this way gradually coming to see her more as she actually is; neither wholly good nor wholly bad, even should she be preponderantly a mother of the one kind rather than the other.

Although his mother is of such great importance to the child, she does not remain the only person in his life for long, because his horizon soon widens and while he is still very young it is necessary for him to admit other people into his life—for instance, his father, and his brothers and sisters. Thus his world is changed and probably he had preferred it as it was before, just himself and his mother together; for it seems that his sense of inner security is inevitably somewhat shaken as he discovers the existence of other members of the family circle, because he tends to feel that his mother is abandoning him in their favour. So for a time he is inclined to be jealous of them. But if his relationship with his mother is on the whole one of warmth and confidence, he will be able to believe that she continues to love him while loving other people at the same time, and thus he becomes able to share her with them instead of needing to have her all to himself. This is an important step towards growing up emotionally in that it paves the way for a degree of security in subsequent relationships, which is essential if they are to be in any degree satisfying and rewarding.

It is through these early family relationships that the first triangular situation of life arises—that of the child, his mother, and his father, and those who have absorbed the truths of Greek mythology will realize why psycho-analysis uses the phrase "Oedipus Complex" to describe it. Its importance lies in the fact that the feelings it evokes will tend in some measure to be re-experienced in other and later triangular situations with which it is associatively linked. This means that the child who fails to establish a reasonably satisfactory relationship with his father and mother in the first place is likely to become the individual for whom every triangular situation tends to be fraught with frustration and anxiety, whereas the child who has been more fortunate in his relationship with his parents will be able as he grows older to meet these situations with confidence rather than dismay. It can therefore be said that whatever may be the child's emotional experiences in the Oedipus situation it sets the stage, as it were, for every other triangular situation that subsequently comes his way, this always in some degree reflecting the relationship he had with his parents in his early days.

As the child comes to relinquish his infantile dependency on his parents through a relationship with them that affords him sufficient inner security to be able to do so, he begins to relate himself increasingly to people and to become in some measure self-determining and self-reliant. At the same time he is inclined to admire his parents and other grown-ups whom he is disposed to see in somewhat the same light, so that, although he has a variety of feelings towards them, he wants, with part of him, to resemble them and to be the kind of child of whom he believes they approve, the foundations thus being laid for the standards he will later come to hold as right and proper for himself, and by which he will seek to order his life. Moreover, in the course of time and provided he is fortunate in being able to grow up in a relatively benign atmosphere, his primitive impulses gradually become channelled in ways that on the whole are acceptable to others as well as to himself—in other words, they become sub-limated. Thus, step by step, and on the basis of confident relationships with those who cared for him in infancy and during the first few years of childhood, social relationships become possible for him, whereas without this basis they would hardly be within his reach.

If he is to become a social being in the fullest sense, there is a further step that has to be taken; he has to develop a conscience—that inner guide and mentor that causes the individual to experience guilt when he offends against his own inner sense of rectitude and in the main promotes behaviour acceptable to others as well as to himself. The psychological mechanisms concerned in this aspect of growing up are highly complex. What chiefly needs to be realized is that the establishment of conscience is directly linked with the meaning authority has for the child through his relationships with his parents and perhaps also with other grown-ups who look after him, since to begin with they necessarily order and control his life. It is only gradually that authority, in whatever terms he sees it, becomes set up inside him as conscience, and psycho-analysis has shown that in this new form it has the peculiarity of being more strict than the external parental authority it supersedes—a fact that helps to explain why it is always in the child's interest to be able to grow up in a tolerant and kind milieu, since a preponderantly punitive one places him at the risk of being dominated throughout his life by a conscience that tends to be excessively harsh and punishing. For instance, the child who finds authority to be rigid and unloving is likely to become the kind of person who tends to be dogged by a sense of wrong-doing and who is therefore unable readily to enjoy such good things as come his way because he doubts whether he deserves them—a doubt that may exist consciously or unconsciously or in both ways at the same time. While, on the one hand, such an individual is usually somewhat of a kill-joy because of a tendency to require of his fellows the same rigid standards he demands of himself, he may on the other hand tend to rebel against all authority as though trying to convince himself that it is not his concern.

At this juncture it would seem appropriate to refer briefly to the individual in whom effective conscience appears to have failed to develop, the delinquent who unconsciously tends to call down punishment upon his head by repeating his offence or committing others being a case in point. It is sometimes postulated that what is happening deep down in his mind, is that while his anti-social behaviour may be prompted by a variety of motives, it is likely to be prompted as well by an unconscious need to assuage guilt that is repressed, and which he is unable to resolve; therefore he continues to get himself into trouble and punishment fails to reform him. This is a tenable idea since feelings that are repressed and therefore unconscious always have a compelling force and influence behaviour in many ways, some of which are socially desirable, others the reverse. It has to be realized however that only as guilt is present in the form of conscience so that the individual is aware of it, can it enable him appropriately to experience remorse for wrong doing and to try deliberately to mend his ways.

Let us now turn to the child who sees authority outside himself as on the whole kindly as well as controlling, and in whom therefore a conscience becomes established that is not unduly harsh and severe.

He may be expected to become the kind of person who is able appropriately to experience guilt and remorse for the faults he recognizes in himself and to be able as well to tolerate the shortcomings he sees from time to time in his fellows, without necessarily condoning them. For the individual who on the whole is disposed to be merciful towards

22

himself is the one who is able to feel kindly towards others, there being thus a special sense in which "charity begins at home".

It has been said that the ways in which the individual is prone to feel towards others, and to himself in relation to them, are rooted in attitudes that became established in him through his early emotional experiences with people, particularly his parents. Thus it is true to say that in a certain way each individual remains in some degree the child of his past—perhaps the child who was always seeking satisfactions that eluded him or perhaps the child who felt that on the whole his needs were met. In other words, no one is completely mature emotionally, the difference between people as individuals being in this respect one of degree only. Fortunately, however, most people become sufficiently adult to be able on the whole to cope adequately with their responsibilities and to establish relationships that are reasonably satisfactory. And this means that there are many more good parents than bad ones—that is to say, parents who are able to afford their children the warm and loving care that makes growing up possible.

And now to turn to the consideration of certain familiar parental attitudes that on the one hand are inimical to the child's satisfactory emotional growth and development and on the other hand serve to promote it. There is for instance the mother whose attitude might be expressed in words such as "my child will not love me unless I respond to his demands without delay—in fact, were I not to do so I should be a bad mother". Obviously she cannot tolerate the crying of her child and is consequently impelled to supply his every need immediately. It may safely be conjectured that in her own early childhood her demands were met in such a way as to cause her to feel that her own mother denied her everything, so that in later life she does not wish to resemble her; con-

23

sequently, when she herself becomes a mother, she identifies with her child: she seeks to meet his needs immediately as she feels hers were not met in earlier days, in this way attempting, vicariously and of course unconsciously, to satisfy through him her own residual feelings of rejection. In contrast is the mother who appears unmoved when her child cries and who perhaps is unconsciously expressing the attitude "children other than myself receive too much attention; I never had what I wanted from my mother, therefore I will not give in to this child's demands on me"; or perhaps she is unconsciously expressing the attitude, "the demands of this child will exhaust me as I feel my greedy and destructive demands exhausted my mother in her attempts to meet them; therefore I will not give in to this child's demands on me". In this instance it may be conjectured that, on the basis of early unsatisfying emotional experiences, the mother is identifying with her own mother ("I may be exhausted") and also with herself as a child ("I will exhaust my mother") and that, because she is so greatly tied to these infantile attitudes, she is now impelled to act them out unwittingly on her own child. In other words, because unconsciously she is still too much her mother's baby, she is not able in real life to be her own child's relatively grown up mother and consequently cannot afford him the confident relationship with her that he needs. In contrast is the attitude of the mother who is more mature emotionally and who therefore does not have to sacrifice herself to her child or her child to herself, but instead is able to care for him lovingly without having to give in to his every whim. It can be inferred that she was once the small child whose mother cared for her in such a way as to cause her to have feelings that in the main were satisfying, with the result that in later life she is not impelled to seek them, vicariously and unconsciously, through her relationship with her child.

The significance of maternal attitudes has hitherto been

stressed because to begin with his mother is the all important person in the child's life. But when the period of complete dependency on her is past and his father increasingly enters into the picture, it is obvious that paternal attitudes also take on considerable importance; for his father too will feel and behave towards him in ways that are more helpful or less so, depending on the degree of emotional maturity he himself has attained. For instance, should feelings of insecurity, first experienced in relation to those who composed the family circle of his early days, persist in him unduly, perhaps because his parents were over-indulgent, or the reverse, it will not be possible for him in every sense adequately to carry the responsibilities of husband and father, because he will be too much the child of his past to be able to do so. It may be, for example, that he tends to see his wife very much in the light of his mother by whom perhaps he felt rejected, and his children in the light of the little brothers and sisters of whom, maybe, he used to feel jealous because it seemed to him that they received more than their fair share of attention. Or again there is the father whose early emotional experiences have on the whole been fortunate and who in consequence is relatively grown up emotionally; he is likely then to see people more or less as they actually are rather than in a distorted way because of residual infantile feelings and attitudes. He will then probably be wise in his selection of a partner and bring into his home life a measure of kindly control and serenity that augurs well for the future of his children; and a mother with a comparable background is likely, of course, to do the same.

Although it can be conjectured that disturbed relationships are not as widely prevalent throughout the community as is suggested by the frequency with which they can be seen to be playing a part in the problems and difficulties of clients, there is no doubt that they help to account for a great deal of unhappiness and frustration both in children and adults generally.

Perhaps the effectiveness of casework in every field will be facilitated as there comes to be a more widespread awareness among caseworkers of the factors that make for healthy growth and development in childhood, together with a growing ability to use this knowledge in work with individuals. This will be the subject considered in the following chapters.

CHAPTER 3

Meeting the Client

The aim of the previous chapters has been to show the importance of understanding how people grow and develop emotionally and that it is their early relationships and experiences that tend to influence their later attitudes and behaviour. It has been stressed that, because a vigorous part of mental life lies below the level of consciousness, some knowledge of unconscious mental processes and their effect on behaviour is necessary for the understanding of people and their problems. And because it is through relationships that it becomes possible to gain insight into the feelings and thoughts of others, this chapter will be concerned with ways in which these become expressed and revealed in the course of client-worker relationships.

It has always been the aim of caseworkers when meeting people who are in trouble to try to convey to them through the warmth with which they are received that they are in the presence of someone who is prepared to listen to their difficulties carefully and with sympathy, so that problems can be unfolded without fear of blame or misunderstanding. In this way a relationship can come into being that enables

27

them to feel free to tell their story in their own manner and at their own pace. A relationship that gives this sense of freedom often provides a new and welcome experience to those who are in distress and forms the beginning of the helping process. But, whereas caseworkers have always recognized to some extent the importance of the relationship, relatively little attention has been paid in the past to the dynamic nature of the feelings that come into activity when one person meets another and to the origin and nature of such feelings. To understand these matters it is necessary, as has been said, to turn to the findings of psycho-analysis, which have immense importance not only for those who are engaged in psycho-analysis or formal psychotherapy, but to those in any field who are working with people.

It has been shown for instance that when people meet, the feelings each has towards the other are not aroused solely by the immediate meeting and occasion, but are always associatively linked with former experiences; in other words present feelings contain within them reflections of the past. Thus it can be said that all the time, and often quite unconsciously, the past is being revived and re-lived in the present. This characteristic of human behaviour which, whether recognized or not, occurs in every relationship, was first observed and conceptualized by Freud, who in his work with patients became aware that feelings of love or the reverse that they were experiencing towards him in the course of analytic treatment, were similar to feelings they had formerly experienced in their relationships with people who had been important to them in their early lives. And because he realized that these feelings were transferred to him from their original objects in infancy or early childhood, he used the term "transference" to describe this particular phenomenon. In psycho-analysis the various manifestations of transference, as they arise in the course of treatment, are used in very

28

special ways, which will be briefly described at this point.

Broadly speaking, the object of psycho-analysis is to help patients to become released from infantile feelings and attitudes by which they are unconsciously dominated. For this purpose a patient is encouraged and permitted, within the confines of the consulting room, to re-live his early emotional experiences, the analyst coming to stand, for the time being, as the representative of those persons in his life who first aroused his feelings of love and hate. It is these feelings that are brought into consciousness and are analysed and interpreted, as they are played out in the relationship, with the object of helping the patient to recognize their primitive and unrealistic nature. This process helps to dispel or modify them, so that he is no longer at their mercy and in consequence is able to develop a more mature attitude both to himself and to others.

Work of this kind requires a deep understanding of the unconscious and its manifestations, and necessitates the use of interpretative methods that are highly specialized. But, as has been said earlier, the recognition and understanding of feelings and attitudes transferred from the past can be extremely helpful to caseworkers because of the deeper insight it gives, even though the use of such understanding is necessarily different to that of the psycho-analyst. It is not the worker's purpose, for instance, to try to trace to their sources in the experience of infancy the feelings and attitudes that the relationship with a client may arouse, nor to encourage the re-living of them in the way described above; even were she professionally qualified to carry out these tasks, the setting in which she works would render her attempts unsuccessful. While this is so, when meeting a client, awareness that some of the feelings he is experiencing in what has been aptly described as "the here and now" of the relationship are, in fact, transferred from the past, can often help to explain their presence, why they are so keenly felt, and that in fact they are not wholly realistic but are in part the offspring of earlier feelings, which have become un-consciously revived through the immediate relationship. And in casework, because of her helping role, the worker will often represent to the client important people in his life, such as his parents or others to whom he turned in childhood at times of need, and be likely therefore to arouse and to draw upon herself feelings that are somewhat similar in quality and kind to those experienced then. Thus he will regard her not only as the person she really is, but also as the person who, by reason of these transferred feelings, he tends to imagine her to be. Awareness of this ever present factor of transference can thus often help to explain a client's feelings, attitudes, or behaviour, which otherwise might seem strange, unrealistic, or inappropriate to the occasion. For instance undue demandingness on a client's part or difficulty in tolerating necessary delays in receiving help, can often be more readily understood and sympathetically accepted if it is recognized that these feelings may spring less from the urgency of need and more from fear lest, like people in his earlier life, the worker will be likely to deny him what he wants or to give only under pressure. Or again, extreme diffidence in asking for help, however pressing the need may be, may reflect past uncertainties regarding the readiness of people to help him, whereas a client whose experiences have led him to believe in the possible helpfulness and kindliness of people is likely to be more able to wait or to accept denial without undue sense of frustration or distress.

It is not always easy to detect these reflections from the past in the course of casework or to be certain what they are representing, and undoubtedly there will always be much that takes place in a relationship that will escape attention or elude understanding, however perceptive a worker may be.

30

But there are occasions when the playing out of transferences is clear to see. It may then be helpful to draw a client's attention to what is actually taking place, with the aim of enabling him to realize whence these feelings have come, so that elements of unrealism or misconceptions that are entering into the relationship may be brought into the open and discussed. The following is an example:

Example of Transference

A client who had been discussing in a previous interview the distress her father's ill-temper had always caused her and who had been very critical of him on this account, opened the next interview with the remark that last week's discussion had been helpful. She then hesitated, obviously having something on her mind that she was reluctant to discuss until the worker asked her what was bothering her. Looking rather anxiously at the worker, the client then replied that she had been wondering during the week whether her comments about her father "might get round to him in some way". In response to this remark the worker said that for some reason it seemed difficult for the client to believe that all that took place at the agency was confidential and asked her why this might be. The client then described several occasions when people had "let me down" and made mischief in the family by repeating things, adding that this was why she had felt so worried after last week's visit.

Here was an instance when feelings from the past were being transferred upon the worker, causing this woman to endow her with the alleged unreliable qualities of her relatives. It is likely, of course, that the feelings of uncertainty regarding the worker's reliability sprang not only from actually remembered experiences, but from others which lay in the long

31

forgotten past. But to these deeply hidden memories the worker had no access. Her concern, however, was with those the client was experiencing at the moment in the "here and now" of the relationship, for it was these that were troubling her and preventing the free expression of her feelings and thoughts.

Capacity to relate to her Client

Although the instance just described provides a relatively simple example of transference, from which it was possible to form some idea of the persisting effects of the client's early experiences, as has already been said it is often by no means easy to discern or to understand what the relationship is revealing. To do so, however partially, requires a real appreciation of the ever-present influence of the unconscious in determining attitudes and behaviour, together with a sound knowledge of the way human beings grow and develop emotionally and how, as described in the previous chapter, the relationships of infancy and childhood can affect the growing personality. It is insight derived from these sources that makes it possible to recognize the play of unconscious activity in the course of a relationship, and so to be able to build up, from what is observed or what is said, some impressions of his past that can help to explain a client's present attitudes and behaviour, which might otherwise remain obscure. To be able to listen in this way calls for a quality of repose in the self that makes quiet, reflective listening possible; listening, which in itself gives an assurance of warm interest and concern, yet allows at the same time for attention to be paid to the client's narrative and to those evidences of feeling so often unconsciously revealed by attitude, gesture, or tone of voice as he pursues his train of thought. To relate to a client in this quiet yet lively way requires as well a capacity to identify with him, so that, to some extent at least, ıt becomes possible to view his problems as he sees them. A generosity of mind, an absence of prejudice or partiality and a ready sympathy with his difficulties are qualities that alone can bring into being that sense of kinship necessary as the basis of every helping relationship. This responsiveness to people, sometimes known as "empathy", is often the result of an intuitive awareness of unexpressed feelings and thoughts, contact being made in this way not only with conscious feelings but with those that lie below the surface of the mind. Those who possess a capacity for intuitive perceptiveness are fortunate, not only because what is perceived in this way so often proves to be correct, but because this apt responsiveness to the feelings and thoughts of others brings into being a special bond of understanding. None the less, because of the common tendency to project personal feelings and thoughts on to others, it is always necessary to be cautious in placing undue reliance on conclusions or inferences that are based on intuition alone, unless there is objective evidence against which they can be tested.

To enlarge now on the important subject of identification: just because sympathies are likely to be stirred when meeting the problems and anxieties of others, it is sometimes all too easy for the worker to respond inappropriately to a situation which, for reasons deeply within her, arouses her interest or excites her compassion to an extent that makes it difficult to afford a client the support he needs. When this happens the situation may be compared to that arising when someone who cannot swim plunges impetuously into a river to save a drowning person instead of attempting his rescue from the bank, with the result that both are in danger of drowning together. To be able to extend a helping hand to those in difficulty or distress requires, paradoxically enough, a capacity to respond warmly and sympathetically to them and their problems or to their feelings of unhappiness, while remaining, at the same time, sufficiently apart to avoid the risk of adding to difficulties through undue emotional involvement.

Counter-Transference

It is always necessary to remember that, like the client, the worker will be unconsciously influenced by her own feelings and attitudes, that is to say by her counter-transferences, and that unless they are reckoned with and understood they may enter into the situation and take command. It may happen, for instance, that in the course of her work she finds herself so sympathetically disposed towards a client that it becomes difficult, if not impossible, to deny his requests, while another may arouse feelings of hostility that make it hard for her to assess his problem fairly or to offer the help needed. Or again, she may become aware that certain kinds of problems arouse her sympathy more than others; the neglected child may make a greater appeal than the rejected wife, or the delinquent boy engage her interest rather than the law-abiding citizen who has fallen upon hard times. Obviously no one can be strictly impartial or be fully aware of personal biases and prejudices, for to some extent they are always present. What is important, however, is the recognition of this fact, so that the attendant risks are minimized; for self-awareness is a first necessity on the part of those who seek to help others. This is why it is always important to examine, as honestly as conscious understanding permits, occasions in the course of a relationship when positive or negative feelings are aroused that seem to be unduly strong, or again why it may be that certain problems seem so irritating, while others arouse interest and concern. Inevitably blind spots will always remain, but where there are known areas of difficulty, it is important that these be honestly faced, so that ways may be found perhaps of modifying them. It is sometimes thought that preoccupation on a worker's part with her feelings that come into activity in the course of her relationships with clients, amounts to unhealthy indulgence in introspection and brings an element of self-consciousness into her work to the detriment of naturalness and spontaneity. But if introspection leads to knowledge of the self and a deepening of insight it is not unhealthy and its value cannot be denied. For it is a capacity to meet the difficulties of others calmly and without undue emotional involvement that enables support to be given when this is needed and tolerance to be extended to those whose ideas and behaviour are personally unacceptable or difficult to understand.

Observing the Transference or glimpsing the Inner World
With these thoughts in mind concerning the dynamic nature of relationships, it may be useful to consider how this understanding can throw added light on a client and his problems from the first moment of contact, a subject that will bring under review several aspects of a first interview.

It is reasonable to suppose that, just because of its helping role, the agency itself will be, to some extent, unconsciously associated in a client's mind with his real or fantasied parents. Thus as he seeks its help, attitudes of mind engendered by his early experiences with those to whom he has turned at times of need are likely to be called forth, the hopes and fears with which he has come being reinforced by these echoes from the past. This is why it is always useful, from the first moment of a client's arrival, to take note of those evidences of feeling with which his coming is attended. Sometimes indications of what is taking place in his mind may be gained from his demeanour in the relatively informal surroundings of the hall or waiting room before he actually meets the worker. Obviously these fleeting impressions should not be taken solely at their face value, for it may readily be that an appearance of outward calm, or even nonchalance, may be a cover for anxieties he is at pains to hide, and obvious signs of tension could have less significance than at first might be supposed. But, none the less, these evidences of feeling may give some indication of what lies below the surface.

In his turn, and as he makes his first contact with the agency, the way he is received by the worker will be extremely important to the client. For, because he is likely to have come at a time of stress, when perhaps feelings of personal inadequacy and dependency are uppermost in his mind, he may be particularly sensitive to all that takes place and be ready to regard the arrangements for his reception as indications of the worker's attitude to him and his problems. In this connection the importance of making the time of waiting as short as possible need hardly be stressed, or again the relief that can be afforded from the realization, through the way he is received, that whether his coming is unexpected or planned, he is genuinely welcome. There are other relatively small yet important matters that can help to give him confidence; for instance, a reasonably comfortable and orderly office can be reassuring to a client who, by reason of his difficulties, is experiencing feelings of diminished self-esteem, and a sense of friendliness may be more readily conveyed if the chairs are set side by side without the formality of an intervening desk. Apart from the pleasant atmosphere of friendliness likely to be created by this arrangement, it has the value of enabling client and worker to see each other without the embarrassment of being directly vis-à-vis, and at the same time it permits the worker, in an unobtrusive way, to take note as he talks of those all-important indications of feelings that are so often unconsciously revealed, not only by what is actually said but by incidental behaviour. The way in which a client's inner world of thought and fantasy

36

is sometimes played out in apparently trifling ways in the course of an interview is illustrated by the following example.

A woman brought her twelve-year-old son to a child guidance clinic on account of a reading difficulty and was invited to discuss his problem with the psychiatrist. She was dressed in an extremely girlish style and wore her hair in long untidy ringlets, which enhanced the impression she gave of studied youthfulness. On arrival in the psychiatrist's room she refused an offered chair, making straight for one designed for a small child, doing the same when she came later to the worker's room, remarking as she moved towards it, "I always like a little one, at home I have had the arms of the baby's chair cut off now that he has grown out of it", adding with a laugh, "The family call it mother's chair as I always use it." As the discussion developed the significance of this woman's behaviour became evident. Throughout the interview her manner towards the worker was that of a child in the presence of a strict parent to whom deference had to be paid, and her ingenuous accounts of the games and interests she shared with her son gave abundant proof of her unconscious desire to be thought of as a child. It seemed in fact that, despite her conscious wishes that her son should do well at school, part of her was wanting him to remain the little boy with whom she could play on equal terms.

It would be welcome indeed if the underlying meaning of what is expressed by word or deed were always as self-evident as in this instance. But such occasions are rare; it is often only after quiet reflection that the unconscious significance of what has taken place becomes at all clear, and at other times it may remain an enigma. These are inescapable facts, which have to be recognized and faced with due humility.

Asking and Listening

It is usually a casework requirement that a clear and factual account be obtained of a client's problems and the circumstances of his life that may have contributed to them. Yet, sometimes, to interrupt the flow of his thoughts and ideas in order to obtain such material may be unwelcome to client and worker alike, particularly if he is describing matters that, though not immediately pertinent to his problems, reveal other important aspects of himself. Sometimes this difficulty can be overcome, to an extent at least, if an interview is allowed to develop in an unstructured way at first, so that as far as time permits, the client is left free to discuss his feelings and thoughts without interruption, the asking of necessary questions being left until later.

As a client talks it is often helpful to have some questions in mind, such as, "What is it that the client is really wanting?", and "Is the problem that he is describing the sole reason for his coming?"; also, "What is the nature of the feelings that the immediate relationship appears to be arousing, and what do they seem to reveal concerning the way in which people in his past have met him at times of need?" It may be that these questions cannot be answered at once or even for some time, but they may be useful guides to thought which can be pursued through the whole course of the session. And when a client has been given an opportunity to reveal his difficulties as he sees them and at the same time feels assured of the worker's sympathetic understanding, then it becomes a relatively easy matter to ask necessary questions. But there are several ways of doing so. For instance, a question put in such terms as "This must have been difficult for you; will you tell me more about it?" is to weight the question with the subjective thoughts and ideas of the listener, whereas the posing of what is sometimes described as an "open-ended" question such as, "This seems to be troubling you; will you tell me more about it?" leaves the way free for the untrammelled expression of feelings that the situation has induced or is inducing at the moment.

Initiative and Approach

At some point in a first interview there will be certain matters useful for the worker to raise. It is always important, for instance, when a suitable opportunity offers, to learn whether a client has come to the agency on his own initiative or has been urged to do so by someone else. Sometimes it may appear that the distinction in a client's mind between choice and obligation is a fine one, a doctor, a priest, or a friend whose opinion is valued and respected, having urged him to seek help, whereas in other instances a Court Order may have allowed of no option, in which case it is probable that some element of authority will attach to the worker. For this reason, a discussion of this subject can often be fruitful in allaying or dispelling anxieties and misunderstandings, and may provide as well a valuable opportunity for the developing of that sense of partnership and shared purpose without which casework can be of little avail; a partnership which, on the worker's part, consists in offering the client her understanding, knowledge, and skill and on his part in admitting her, as far as he is able, to his confidence.

It is easy to assume sometimes that clients accustomed to depend on others for the solution or relief of their problems, may be unable to respond to an invitation that involves their active participation and a sharing of responsibility. It may well require time and the gradual working through of some of his resistances before a client's real participation is obtained. Experience has shown, however, that even quite limited and unsophisticated people are frequently willing and able to respond, after a time, to a suggestion that indicates the importance attaching to their active cooperation; latent capacities for self-help and self-direction often exist in unexpected quarters, and the skill lies in the worker's ability to call them forth however poorly developed they may be. The opening up of this subject can then lead to a discussion of the services at the agency's disposal and in a general way its methods of work, all of which are matters that concern a client closely and about which he has a right to know, so that he can decide whether or not he wishes to avail himself of its help.

The Client's Reserves

As a client unfolds his story it may become evident that parts of it are particularly charged with feeling, signs of embarrassment or casual or indirect references to matters that are clearly important providing evidence that this is so. It often requires very considerable judgment and discrimination on a worker's part to know whether it is necessary or desirable to approach these sensitive areas. It may be, of course, that it is essential to do so if a problem is to be clarified. There may also be occasions when to leave them aside would result in failure to appreciate the nature of the problem or to obtain material required by a professional colleague. Obviously, to attempt to force a client's confidence would be both harmful to the client and distasteful to the worker. But the fact that a client has referred at all to distressing subjects may well be proof of some desire to discuss them, so if they are quietly and gently approached in a way that shows recognition of their painful nature and respect for his reluctance to discuss them, he may be relieved and grateful at being given an opportunity to do so. There is the further point that diffidence on a worker's part in approaching matters that are obviously weighted with feelings of pain, shame, or anxiety, may impose a barrier between herself and the client, thus inadvertently increasing his uneasiness, an apparent reluctance to refer to them suggesting that his behaviour has indeed set him beyond the pale, hence her silence. So he may leave with disappointment or a sense of rejection or even with reluctance to come again, feeling that she is not in real contact with him or his needs. For instance, a woman who appeared to be calm and relatively undisturbed when referring, almost incidentally, to her husband's recent imprisonment for theft, was manifestly relieved when the worker brought the subject into the open by alluding to the pain and distress it must be causing her despite her apparent courage in facing this difficult and distressing situation. The woman then remarked that she was glad the worker had referred to "my trouble" because somehow or other it made her feel that it was not quite so disgraceful as she had felt it to be when she first came to the agency, adding that she had come fearing to mention it, lest the worker might think little of her in consequence.

Situations in which Casework cannot meet the Problem
There are occasions in the course of casework when it will become evident to the worker that a client's difficulties are such that they demand more knowledge and skill than she possesses. It may not always be easy to accept that this is so, perhaps because such an admission may challenge under-lying feelings of omnipotence, or perhaps identification with the client makes it difficult to face his disappointment or annoyance. Yet to admit to professional limitations may be the only honest course to pursue, for otherwise hopes and expectations may be raised that cannot be fulfilled. Sometimes, of course, there will be other sources of help to which a client can be directed, but if these are not available

41

it can be extremely hard to meet the situation in a way that prevents him from experiencing an undue sense of rejection, particularly if his earlier relationships have caused him to feel that people tend to disregard his needs. Clearly there can be no fully satisfactory answer to a problem of this kind. If, however, the worker is able to discuss his sense of frustration with him, she may at least be able to show him that his disappointment is realized and shared, even if she may not be able to offer him the help he desires.

Termination of Interviews

The termination of an interview is another matter requiring thought and care. How often it can happen, for instance, that a session runs on, if allowed to do so, in a desultory and somewhat meaningless way, or that at the eleventh hour the client raises important points that make it extremely difficult to close the interview without loss of valuable material or without appearing to be discourteous or abrupt. It may be that a client's reluctance to leave is due to a wish to prolong an occasion he finds pleasant, or to an unconscious desire to control the worker, because in part she represents to him a parent whose whole attention he wishes to keep. In this way he may, consciously or unconsciously, try to force her to give him more than his share of her time and interest by leaving the discussion of important matters until the last moment, thus depriving other clients who, in fantasy, may represent to him the rivals of his childhood. Sometimes these difficulties can be avoided if the worker explains that she has a certain time to set at his disposal and that she is sure he will appreciate this, thus encouraging him to face realities and perhaps adding to his sense of partnership, since in this matter, as in others, his cooperation is expected.

Conscious and Unconscious Factors in Communication

Earlier in this chapter attention was drawn to the importance of noting the attitude and general bearing of a client as he discusses his problems, because of the evidences of feeling thus revealed. But as yet little has been said concerning the subject matter he spontaneously raises, or how, from time to time, it may be possible to perceive some of the unconscious meanings that become expressed through what he is saying. This subject presents difficulties because understanding of unconscious behaviour inevitably depends on the degree of insight achieved by each worker, but there are always certain points to bear in mind when listening to a client. Opening remarks, for instance, often give indications of underlying feelings, thoughts, or ideas with which he is preoccupied at the moment, however irrelevant or inconsequent they may appear to be. But if they are later related to other material that is brought into the discussion, their meaning may then become more clear. A comment, for example, about the weather may be consistent with the prevailing climatic conditions, but it may also refer in part to a client's inner climate of feeling; or again, a remark that appears to be but a polite formality may prove to have considerable bearing on a client's problem, as the following instance shows. A young married woman came to an agency ostensibly to consult a worker about a mortgage. Almost at once she remarked, "What wonderful work you welfare people do." As she talked it became evident that her reason for coming lay less in her need for advice and more in her wish to discuss her marital problems, which were distressing her greatly and for which she felt herself largely to blame. It was not until she had discussed her anxieties on this score that the meaning of her opening comment became clear in so far as it referred to the immediate situation. It was evident then that this woman, who felt she had contributed so much to the failure

43

of her marriage, was feeling that she had been a person whose "work" had been anything but wonderful. It seemed likely, therefore, that what she was unconsciously expressing through her opening remark was the wish that she could be a helpful person like the worker, rather than the troublesome individual that so often she felt herself to be.

The Significance of the apparently Irrelevant

It frequently happens too that a variety of subjects is raised by a client with apparently little bearing on the immediate issue. For instance, it may be that he refers during an interview to items of public interest, to people he has met, or to things he has seen that have attracted his attention. It is always useful to wonder why these matters may be in his mind, why they have been selected, as it were, from among many others that might equally have attracted his interest and attention. Whereas it may be possible to account for this, in part at least, on a rational basis, it may seem that the degree of preoccupation with certain subjects suggests that they are of more than passing importance, because in some way they relate to himself and his problems. To give an example: A client who had come to consult an agency about his unhappy relationship with his wife and family, for which he felt they were entirely to blame, commented at once on arrival on the wanton damage the boys of the neighbourhood had inflicted on an adjacent derelict building. He complained of the ineffectualness of the police in preventing such destruction and described the strong measures he would use against the offenders were he in a position of authority. Passing from this subject to his problems with his family, it was noticed that he consistently blamed them for his troubles, to the exclusion of any possibility that he might have contributed to them himself. Paraphrased, the burden of his song was, "Others may do destructive things but I do not," in

44

this way expressing perhaps a life-long tendency to divest himself of all responsibility for wrong doing and to project blame on to others. But his general bearing and his dogmatism suggested that he was not as blameless as he consciously wished to appear. It seemed likely that his interest in the damaged building and his desire for the unruly elements in the community to be punished, gave indication of his own inner anxieties concerning the unruly elements in himself, of which perhaps in the recesses of his mind he was both dimly aware and also afraid. How truly this represented the actual situation became evident later, as the worker came to know both him and his family.

Projection

The above example illustrates not only the importance of paying close attention to the subjects raised by a client, but also to the tendency that exists in people to project on to others faults existing in themselves, thus making them their scapegoats. If this truth is recognized, it will be seen that comments or criticisms made about others usually refer less to the person about whom they are made and more to the one who makes them. The example just given illustrates yet another aspect of the workings of the unconscious mind, which is that when, in the course of an interview, a client mentions other people, his references to them so often relate to the worker and what she happens to be representing to him at the moment. When, for example, in the instance given above the client spoke of the police and the need for them to exert control on the unruly boys whose actions he was deploring, was it not likely that at that moment he was unconsciously making a plea for the worker to take control of those unruly elements in himself of which he was so afraid?

The following example also illustrates the significance of such references: A young woman, who had been discussing her shortcomings as a wife and mother, complained of the absence of privacy on the Council estate in which she lived, remarking that the house next door was so close to her own that her neighbour could "look right into my kitchen", adding that this woman always seemed to do so when it was in a muddle. In this context it would not be unreasonable to conjecture that despite her apparent readiness to discuss her personal difficulties, the client was feeling as well some resentment towards the worker who, like her neighbour, had come close enough to her to be able to see "the muddle" within herself, which, at least in part, she would have preferred to hide.

Though, as will be shown in the next chapter, it is always necessary in the course of casework to be discriminating in interpreting to a client the unconscious significance of what he is saying, awareness of the inner meaning of the material is always helpful in throwing light on the client himself and on his difficulties.

These few examples will have served their purpose if they have shown the importance, stressed earlier, of careful, thoughtful listening to all that a client says and the attuning of the ear to the themes that so often, like a connecting thread, link together the apparently chance remark, the casual reference, or the account of circumstances or events which at the moment appear to be occupying his thoughts, recognizing that the material so often conveys a hidden message. It is easy, of course, to jump to conclusions without sufficient evidence to support them, or to bend material to satisfy some preconceived idea existing in the worker's mind rather than in the client's. There is no real safeguard against these risks, other than knowledge of unconscious processes and self-awareness. These can help to modify or eliminate the all important influence of counter-transferences, which otherwise may prevent access to a client's feelings and block the way to an understanding of his problems, because the worker's own feelings stand in the way. The ways in which the realization of the dynamic nature of relationships and awareness of unconscious activity can be of value in the ordinary course of casework will be discussed in the next chapter.

CHAPTER 4

The Helping Process

To meet and to try to help people who are in trouble is a task that calls for those qualities of perceptiveness and sympathetic understanding to which reference was made in the last chapter. Because the personality and character of the caseworker is important, it is appropriate before discussing ways in which help can be offered to clients, to consider briefly some of the desirable qualities, in terms of character and personality, of those who seek to help their fellow men. The transference and counter-transference elements in relationships have already been considered, but little has been said as yet regarding those personal qualities on which the value of casework so greatly depends, for what the worker proves to be as a person often matters far more to clients than anything she may try to do on their behalf. In considering this subject it would seem that personal integrity, with all that it implies of frankness and straightforwardness in meeting and dealing with people, is a quality that must be reflected in every aspect of her work, difficult as it may be from time to time to meet helpfully the demands imposed by truthfulness and honesty. It would seem too that work with people who are in need or distress must always be undertaken in a spirit of humility, induced by a breadth of understanding of human nature and its frailties, combined with a lively sense of personal limitations and failure, making it possible in all sincerity to subscribe to the thought, "There but for the grace of God go I". It is this attitude of mind that permits of the development of the sense of kinship between client and worker referred to in the last chapter. But perhaps the most valuable quality a worker can bring to her clients is that which springs from a mind at ease and harmonious within itself; a mind in which tension and strain are at a minimum because her own emotional difficulties have been resolved or modified so that the problems of clients can be met in an unprejudiced way. It is this that constitutes the helping and healing element in relationships with people.

In the following pages some of the practices and skills of casework and the thinking on which they are based will be reviewed in some detail, examples being given to illustrate the use of the dynamic factors in relationships.

Limitations of Reassurance

Because clients who come to casework agencies usually do so at times of stress, it is appropriate to consider in general terms effective and helpful ways of meeting their immediate anxieties. It is sometimes difficult, as has been pointed out earlier, to combine ready sympathy for the distresses of others with a degree of detachment that is supporting and strengthening. This may be because a client's particular troubles touch off certain subjective feelings in the worker so that, in effect, anxiety is met with anxiety. For this reason, or because it is so difficult to tolerate the sufferings of others without trying to relieve them, it is often tempting to offer reassurance before the facts of the situation are really known. But this may not be a wise or helpful thing to do because, unless there are obvious grounds for offering encouragement and hope, to try to reassure is likely in the end to add to distress rather than to relieve it. If, for instance, reassurance is extended prematurely, it may seem to the troubled person that the reasons for his anxiety and concern cannot have been fully realized, for otherwise why should it be assumed that they could so readily be charmed away? By contrast, to relate to the troubles and anxieties of others without seeking in any way to minimize or play them down is often the surest way of affording relief, for this gives comforting proof that they have been understood at least to some extent and suggests that they may not be as serious as formerly imagined, since they are being discussed in this direct and dispassionate way. The occasion mentioned in the last chapter, when a woman was relieved by the worker's reference to her husband's prison sentence, is a case in point.

Problems concerning Advice
The seeming impossibility of directly giving reassurance brings to the fore the related question of advice-giving and the extent to which this can be of value. As every caseworker knows, advice is constantly and understandably asked for by those who come to social agencies, because these organizations exist very largely for the purpose of advising people on a wide variety of matters. Without making the line of demarcation too precise, generally speaking it is justifiable to distinguish between advice on matters of fact and on matters of opinion, the former calling for resourcefulness in knowing where to find the required information, the latter demanding knowledge of the applicant and the reasons that have led him to ask for it. But, despite this distinction, it is always important to be aware of the possibility that even when factual information is sought, the client's visit may also have been prompted by other needs. This points to

the usefulness of always keeping in mind the questions posed in the last chapter, as to the reasons that have brought a client to an agency, so that this possibility is not overlooked.

The question of advice-giving also challenges thought, because, even when asked for and accepted in all sincerity, it is so rarely followed. This may be due to several reasons: perhaps the advice offered proves to be unsuitable when tried, or perhaps when accepted intellectually, emotional factors make it unacceptable. Or it may be that despite a request for advice the applicant has already decided on a line of action, which he never really intended to relinquish, or he may be a vacillator who, while accepting it, is likely to reject it when faced with a decision. There are also times when advice is asked for and apparently accepted, but because of some unconscious need to prove it wrong, it is followed in a way that inevitably causes it to fail. For example, a strict father who was extremely hostile to his adolescent son, was advised by a worker to give the boy more freedom than he had formerly been allowed. The father appeared to agree that this was advisable, but in carrying out this suggestion he lifted all normal restraints, allowing the boy to come and go as he wished, with the result that the lad, who was quite unused to so much freedom, was soon quite out of hand. The father then came to the agency to criticize the worker for the advice given, placing the blame for what had happened upon her shoulders and remarking, "Now you know what my son is like!" It is always necessary to be aware as well of the possibility that in offering advice the worker may draw upon herself feelings attaching to authority figures in the client's past on whom he relied for guidance and direction, so that in some degree he may be thrust back into a position of dependency, if it is made too easily available. This is why it is always so necessary to allow time for thorough discussion of the problem on which help is asked, in order to put before the

51

client possible alternatives, leaving him to make his choice. This may sometimes seem a tedious process to a client who wants quick and ready answers to his problem, but short cuts often prove to be the longest way home. The following describes an occasion when advice was requested in no uncertain terms; it also shows some of the difficulties that would have resulted had it been as readily given.

A young and obviously intelligent mother came to a child guidance clinic to ask for help with her son John, aged $3\frac{1}{2}$. He was the elder of two children and was proving to be extremely difficult to manage. The family had recently come to the district and the mother gave this as a reason that had induced her to come for help, saying that she had no relatives or friends to whom she could now turn for advice. She seemed to be extremely worried over John's disobedience and jealousy of his little sister, feeling that her bad management was responsible for the child's behaviour. She made it clear that she had come, as she put it, to find someone who would "tell me what to do".

On her first visit she described her mother in glowing terms, saying how "marvellous" she was with children and how good she had been with John when he was a baby. It was quite evident that this young mother was expecting to find in the worker a "parent" who would be as helpful as the child's grandmother was alleged to have been. It was also evident that the mother was an extremely anxious woman who had little faith in her own maternal capacities. This was shown by remarks such as, "You people must know all about children" and again, "You are the experts". She also repeatedly asked for advice on specific points of management—"What should I do when John hits his sister?", "Is it all right to smack children when they are naughty?", and so on. It was quite difficult, in the face of these questions, to withstand the mother's pleas for immediate advice or to avoid being cornered into giving it. But to have offered it would certainly have tended to confirm her anxieties concerning her inability to manage her child. At the same time the mantle of the grandmother who was so "marvellous" with children would most surely have descended upon the worker had she met the mother's demands without delay. And this would certainly have been unfortunate for, as was revealed later, despite the glowing picture that had been painted of the grandmother, her dominating and interfering ways had often irritated the mother. In view of this, what might have resulted had the worker been swept into offering advice is not difficult to imagine! But instead of doing this, the worker tried to help this anxious mother to see that, despite her certainty that the worker knew the answers, this was not the case, and that careful thought was required, in which she needed to participate, so that together they could discover how best the help she was so urgently desiring could be given.

The pressure of clients for advice is equalled sometimes by their wish to obtain approval of ideas they hold or of behaviour that may be difficult to support on ethical grounds. It is not easy sometimes to know how to respond on such occasions, particularly if opinion is invited before there has been time in which to come to know a client and to understand some of the reasons that underlie the thoughts or actions in question. Obviously, how he feels, thinks, and acts will be partly governed by the unconscious, and so he may not be receptive at the moment to another point of view. "All that they say or do is their truth, so why am I angry?"[1] contains a philosophy that, if sincerely held, may make it possible to meet the views and actions of another person with

[1] MOORE, GEORGE. *Héloïse and Abelard.* London, 1921.

tolerance, the way then being left open for questionable or debatable matters to be discussed later, should opportunity arise. And this may readily come, if the client feels assured of the worker's open-mindedness; the very fact that he seeks support for his views and actions suggests that some doubts concerning them lurk below the surface, because approval is not generally asked when certainty exists. And this aspect of his questioning can often profitably be raised in terms that help him to become aware that his underlying uncertainty has been recognized and that it is *this* that it would be fruitful to discuss. There are other more difficult occasions when in the face of a painful or difficult situation a client, with full intent, deceives or misleads someone else and then asks for support or approval of his action. It may be impossible on ethical or commonsense grounds to condone or to justify his behaviour. And just because the client's desire to seek sanction for what he is doing is so often the outcome of doubts in his own mind regarding the course he is pursuing, he is likely to be very sensitive to criticism and ready to project his own uncertainties on to the worker. So he may be on the defensive before there has been time for an impartial discussion of the matter in question; a situation to which the worker may contribute, if in fact she is as disapproving as with part of himself he believes her to be. These situations are likely to test out the worker's counter-transferences because, unless they are under control, she will be unable to view his difficulties in the unprejudiced way that may ultimately enable him to reconsider his course of action. The following occasion shows how a worker's personal feelings held sway to the detriment of her relationship with the client.

The father of a family of four children, the eldest of whom was a backward boy of twelve, was charged with committing a serious theft, to which he ultimately confessed.

54

While waiting to be tried he was remanded in custody. The building he had raided was close to the school attended by his eldest boy and the child was likely at some point to hear of his father's misdeeds from his schoolmates or others in the neighbourhood, but his mother was trying to convince herself that all the children could be kept in ignorance of what had happened. When visited by a caseworker, the mother knew that the father would inevitably go to prison, but was indulging in many lies and subterfuges in order to maintain the fiction to the children that their father was working at a job away from home. The mother sought the worker's approval of this plan. Though it was impossible to support it either on ethical or realistic grounds, the mother's pathetic attempt to protect her husband by a virtual denial of his guilt was evident enough; this was the only way, mistaken as it seemed, in which she could meet a situation that was causing her such intolerable suffering and shame. But the worker's sense of rectitude was offended, so that when her opinion was asked, instead of discussing the situation dispassionately with the aim of helping the mother to see the fallacies of her plan and her underlying uncertainties about it, she at once became the critic and so forfeited her helping role. Although the worker met the mother on two other occasions, she never showed any desire to discuss the matter again and it was not until concealment became impossible, because the father had received a two-year prison sentence, that the mother told the children the truth.

Problems of Dependency

Another matter likely to arise in casework, which merits discussion, is the tendency on the part of clients to become dependent in the course of a helping relationship. This tendency, which may show itself in many ways, is sometimes a matter of concern to a worker, lest it should become unduly strong or too firmly fixed. But anxiety on this score may be unjustified, because when a person turns to another at a time of stress, for a while at least dependence on the helping person is both natural and inevitable. It is important, however, that this tendency should be recognized as it arises, for if it is allowed unhealthy and unchecked growth, capacities for independence may be weakened. Sometimes indeed undue fears in this direction result in the overlooking of some of the positive values that a period of dependence can offer. For instance, if a client has never enjoyed a warm and satisfying relationship with his own parents, he may be greatly helped by a relationship with a worker who, in the manner of a good parent, is prepared to accept for a time his desire to depend on her. Such a relationship can also provide a valuable opportunity for the playing out by a client of other emotional needs left unsatisfied by the experiences of the past. To give a common example: A woman who had grown up in very adverse circumstances, in which her affectional needs had rarely been met, became for a time extremely dependent on the worker to whom she had turned for help with a difficult problem in relation to her husband. She came very regularly to the agency and for a time consulted the worker on every conceivable issue that had arisen in the course of the previous week, whether this concerned her immediate problem or her everyday life. It seemed, in fact, as if in the manner of a child, she needed to obtain sanction and approval for all that she did. This was frequently brought to the woman's notice in some such terms as, "Do you see how much you want me to be a mother to you, who, unlike your own, will guide and direct you in all that you do?" Time was required for her to work through some of these feelings, but gradually she became able to relinquish the somewhat infantile attitude she had been adopting towards the worker, thus allowing her common sense and judgment to come into play. *Reculer pour mieux sauter* describes very aptly and succinctly what, at best, may result from a relationship in which such feelings are recognized and wisely met.

There are other clients whose need to depend springs from weakness of character and personality, which makes them ever ready to rely on anyone who is prepared to think and act for them. It cannot be denied that caseworkers sometimes become the ready prey of such persons, their helplessness and inability to arrange their affairs arousing compassion to an extent that makes it difficult to refrain from rushing to their aid without allowing sufficient time to come to know them and the facts of the situation. Sometimes, too, zeal in going to the rescue may be the outcome of some hidden desire for power on the worker's part, for which the management of other people's affairs offers scope and satisfaction. Their difficulties seem to provide justification for so doing, detrimental as this sometimes may be to such capacities for self-help and independence as they possess.

Short-Contact Casework

It is sometimes easy to overlook the importance of the relationship when a client makes temporary or fleeting use of the services of an agency. Yet often enough these seemingly casual contacts can be of considerable help to a client if they are used with insight. His coming in respect of some relatively trivial matter may be a cover for another difficulty which he may be reluctant at first to discuss, his visit being very largely for the purpose perhaps of discovering the kind of reception he is likely to be accorded. This again points to the importance of bearing in mind the question posed in the last chapter, "What is it that the client is really wanting?", together with the related one, "Is the problem he is describing the sole reason for his coming?" For, as has been said, it is often easy to be misled by the apparent need and so overlook another, which underlies it. And when it seems that the underlying reasons for the client's coming are evident, it is useful to make this known to him, this in itself often bringing the relief of knowing that his difficulty has been recognized; but whether or not he wishes to discuss it is a matter that should be left to him to decide. Other clients may seek an agency's help because of a need for a personal relationship with someone who is warm and friendly, to whom they can feel able to confide their feelings of loneliness, discouragement, or defeat. To meet a need of this kind is a form of help that from time immemorial caseworkers have felt privileged to offer, providing in this way one of the most valuable services they can render to the community. Then again a client may come to discuss some matter that is perplexing him; he may not ask for or want specific advice, preferring to use the occasion for the purpose of "thinking aloud" in the presence of someone on whom he feels he can rely for sympathetic yet impartial interest. As every caseworker knows, it sometimes requires considerable patience and self-restraint to stand aside, as it were, in order to allow a client freely to discuss his feelings and thoughts in this way. It is often helpful on these occasions to summarize, at some point, what has been said, doing so in some such terms as, "This is what you have been telling me" or again, "These are some of the conclusions you seem to have come to", so that shape and design is given to the feelings and thoughts he has been expressing. And so he may come to see his difficulties afresh, through the opportunity he has been allowed for reflection and the crystallizing of his ideas.

For instance, a mother became able to see for herself, through talking matters over in this way, that her adolescent son's demands for greater freedom were in fact consistent with his age and interests and that her reluctance to accede to them was to a large extent the result of her own jealous wishes for him to remain her dependent child. To take another example:

A woman who shared her home with a younger sister became aware, as she described their difficulties, that some of the enmity that existed between them was due less perhaps to the younger girl's unreasonableness and more to the feelings of resentment the older sister bore to their mother, who, when alive, had always been indulgent to this younger daughter. The worker listened quietly and attentively to what the older woman had to say, merely playing back to her, from time to time in the words that had been used, the description of the situation she had given. Towards the end of the session the older woman remarked, quite spontaneously, that perhaps her sister was not as responsible for the unhappiness at home as she had hitherto supposed.

These two examples suggest that both clients had come to the agency at a time when some uneasiness existed in themselves concerning the part they were playing in their respective problems. Probably they were not consciously aware of this, but through the opportunity they were given to use the occasion on their own ways, they came to perceive and in some measure to accept that some of the difficulties they were experiencing were due to their own attitudes rather than to those of others.

For whatever reasons clients seek casework help, whether because of conscious difficulties or for others of which they are less aware, it is likely that many come in the first instance with a desire to release feelings of anxiety or distress and a wish to find someone in the nature of a good parent who, they hope, will be responsive to them and their needs. And sometimes an opportunity for the freeing of pent-up feelings of this kind is all that the client wants or can accept at the moment, even though it may be apparent to the worker that his problems justify further and perhaps prolonged help. It is sometimes difficult in such circumstances to refrain from exceeding the client's mandate, but if the relationship has been one that, however brief, has proved its value to him, he will be likely to come again for further discussions at a time of his own choosing.

Supportive Casework

This discussion so far has centred on some of the ways in which clients can receive help through a relationship in which the worker's role is outwardly, and to some considerable extent, a passive one, her contribution being largely that of a sympathetic and discerning listener. But now more direct and active ways of offering help will be considered, which, like those already discussed, are sometimes possible within the "here and now" of a helping relationship.

It is a common experience in casework to meet clients whose self-respect and self-confidence are sadly lacking because of the actual adversities that have brought them to the agency. Among them, however, there will always be some whose early experiences have given little opportunity to develop those qualities of personality and character that might have enabled them to meet the responsibilities of life in a mature and reasonable way. It would be idle to suppose that long standing personality defects or unsatisfactory character formations, which have their roots in the parent-child relationship of long ago, are likely to be changed to an appreciable extent through casework help. Yet experience has shown that, if some of the emotional difficulties of such persons are realized, it can be possible through a casework relationship to provide opportunities for strengthening a weak ego and for fostering emotional growth where infantile attitudes have tended to prevail. The following example shows how some changes took place in a client who had suffered long from feelings of inadequacy and failure, through a relationship in which he was helped to work through some of his emotional difficulties:

A client who was deeply troubled by the unfaithfulness of his wife, whom he was now divorcing, and by the difficulties his unfortunate marriage had caused to himself and his two sons, was extremely self-blaming when, at long last, he sought an agency's help over arrangements for their care. He was extremely diffident on arrival, obviously being apprehensive as to the kind of reception he would be given. He seemed quite surprised by the worker's interest in his problems and by her assumption that marital problems could rarely be ascribed solely to one partner in a marriage. He seemed in fact to be so puzzled by her attitude that she asked him why he thought that he alone was to blame—might it not be that his wife too had behaved badly? But he remained obdurate. Encouraged by her interest, he then told her that after the death of his father when he was seven years old, his mother, who had several other small children to care for, had sent him to a children's home, doing this on the advice of a friend who had convinced her that this would be to his advantage. But to him his mother's action spelt banishment, particularly as his removal from home quickly followed an occasion when a mischievous act had brought down her wrath upon his head. He could never forget, he said, that in her anger she had called him " bad" and had assured him that he would never come to any good.

Since then, although as he told the worker, he had done reasonably well both at school and in the job of his choice, he never felt that he would be really successful or that people would like to trust him, because he felt that some

61

inherent badness in himself would always be likely to let him down. This he thought accounted for the failure of his marriage, for as he put it, if he had been a better man surely his wife would not have left him or been so dissatisfied with everything he tried to do for her. Unsolicited information however from an outside source indicated that the wife was a very childish person who had never been able to accept the responsibilities of marriage and parenthood. Although some practical assistance was given to this man over arrangements for the care of his two children, most of the work was centred on his feelings of defeat and failure and personal unworthiness. At first he came very tentatively to the agency, as though, despite his appointment, the worker might not be prepared for his visit or really want him to come. He was never pressed to do so, being told that while she would be glad to see him if he found his visits helpful, whether he came or not was a matter for him to decide. His difficulty in accepting the worker's readiness to see him was not hard to understand, since for a time she evidently stood for him as a representative of his mother who, in his own mind, whatever the realities of the situation may have been, had sent him away because he was "bad". His aloofness, which persisted for a time, was evidently due to fear of a second rejection on the basis of "once bitten twice shy!"

From time to time he would test out the sincerity of the worker's interest in him by cancelling an appointment without any very good reason and then enquire by phone whether she wished him to come again. On these occasions, which became rarer as time went on, she would reply that, as he knew, she would be glad to give him another appointment, if he so wished. And at his next visit, if it seemed appropriate to do so, she would point out that for some reason he seemed still uncertain of her interest and that perhaps this was because he still felt her to be, in part at least, the mother who had rejected him. Very gradually through the five to six months of their work together, this man came to recognize the existence of some goodness in himself and to realize as well that he possessed capacities and strengths that formerly he would never have admitted. Ultimately, after deciding to change his job and start afresh in a new environment, he obtained a post of considerable responsibility. His selection from a number of applicants gave him great satisfaction and a sense of real achievement.

This example is given chiefly to illustrate the way in which a relationship can be used as a means of ego strengthening, but it also shows how help was given in another direction. The reader is referred at this point to the discussion in the second chapter, which describes how "the inner guide and mentor", in other words the super-ego, comes into being and why, if the influences and experiences of childhood have led to the implantation of ideas and behaviour that are too exacting, the super-ego may be experienced as a severe inner mentor rather than a kindly guide. It will have been apparent that this man was at the mercy of feelings of this kind. An important part of the work with him lay, in fact, in helping him to become aware of the excessively exacting standards of behaviour which he both expected of himself and felt that others demanded of him. Sometimes he would turn to the worker, when such matters arose in the course of the session, and make a comment such as, "You don't seem to think that everyone should be all that perfect", to which she would reply in some such terms as, "Well, you are a human being, are you not?" Although little progress was made in helping this conscience-ridden man to modify these feelings, it is perhaps true to say that some slight easement of them took place.

63

But, for reasons already given, he is always likely to remain over-conscientious and severe with himself. But it can happen sometimes, as in this instance, that through a client's relationship with a worker whom he respects and in whom he has confidence, some slight modification of conscience takes place by gradually taking over from her in the course of a relationship other ideas and values than those he formerly held. This process is one that allows for the gradual introjection by the client of another parent in the person of the worker, who is more sympathetic to human weaknesses and failures than the real or imagined parent of childhood who, in his view, was so demanding of excellence and so intolerant of errors.

This discussion of possible ways of strengthening the ego through a relationship or modifying an over-strict conscience, would be incomplete without reference to the help that may be offered to people whose immaturity of outlook and personal habits suggests that they have never acquired normal social and ethical standards of behaviour. The difficulties presented by these people are only too well known to caseworkers in every field, whether they are met with in separate individuals or in so called "problem families"; for some of them have no desire to change their way of life, which is satisfying enough to them provided they are assured of food and shelter, however unacceptable their habits may be to others. And, even should they desire to change, it is often difficult to know how to help them to do so, since in many respects they are like irresponsible, clamorous children, whose urgency to satisfy a want brooks no denial and whose behaviour is noticeably lacking in restraint or foresight, their attitudes to life giving proof that mentally and emotionally they have never attained the stature of adult men and women. The experience of those who have worked consistently with clients who, in effect, are children disguised as adults, shows that changes can sometimes come about by slowly building up a relationship with them that offers warmth and understanding, thus enabling them gradually to take over from the worker, as they might from a wise and kindly parent, ideas and ways of behaviour never learnt in childhood. The patient work required, and the ability to meet the frequent disappointments and frustrations which are inevitable in the course of it, necessitates particular qualities of tolerance and perseverance in the worker if even limited success is to be obtained. It demands for a time an acceptance free from censure or blame, of the ways of life of the people with whom she is working, the immature attitudes that lie behind their primitive behaviour being recognized and accepted. This attitude of mind is only possible if she has come to terms with her own inner anxieties, so that she can view the chaos and disorder, in which such persons usually live, with a measure of detachment that, until confidence is fully established, contains no hint of reform. This difficult and exacting work is still at the stage of experiment, but for those who are emotionally able to undertake it and possess the required courage, it seems to offer possibilities that justify its further exploration.[1]

Interpretative Casework

In all that has so far been discussed emphasis has been laid on the relationship—how it may be used by clients in various need situations and how it may be a means through which some modification of attitudes can take place. But the direct offering of insight has only been touched upon very briefly, this subject having been left until now because it justifies discussion in some detail. It brings the general question of

[1] For a valuable contribution to this subject, readers are referred to an article by E. E. Irvine entitled "Research into Problem Families" (*British Journal of Psychiatric Social Work*, Vol. 9, 1954).

interpretation under review and particularly the kinds of interpretation that can usefully be made in the course of casework. It is perhaps unfortunate that, for want of a suitable alternative, it is necessary to use the term interpretation to describe the kind of insight-giving communications appropriate to this field of work. This term has been borrowed from psycho-analysis, where it is used to denote the analyst's attempts to bring what is unconscious into consciousness.

Caseworkers have to interpret their client's communications differently and aim at a different level of insight. For, when clients come to a casework agency, they are not asking for analysis, but for help with some problem with which they cannot deal. It will frequently happen, of course, that the work will extend beyond the difficulty on which help is sought, because relatively few problems are the result of fortuitous circumstances alone and, as has been shown in the first chapter, the way in which people meet their difficulties depends very much on the character and personality of each. In consequence, it will often be necessary to help clients become aware of some of the emotional factors that have brought their problems into being or which, without their knowledge, appear to be contributing to them at the moment. The offering of insight by means of interpretations is limited in casework settings, not only because the work is problem-centred, but because the worker's equipment and training and the facilities available to her only permit contact to be made with feelings and thoughts that are near to the threshhold of a client's consciousness, rather than with those deeply hidden in his unconscious mind. But, none the less, relief of tension and anxiety and modification of behaviour can result from them if they are wisely given and rightly timed. This is the crux of the matter, for the offering of insight in a way that is really helpful to clients is not solely contingent upon an ability to read and to understand the language of the unconscious, but also depends upon wisdom and discretion in choosing the moment for its communication. The worker must not be impatient to make a point because to do so is personally gratifying, but should rather await the moment when it seems that the thought or idea that it may be helpful to convey is sufficiently near the surface of a client's mind for him to be likely to receive it. For, although her deeper insight and the fact that she is not emotionally involved in the situation, may often cause a worker to find herself ahead of the client in understanding, it is always necessary when interpreting to seek to be in emotional alignment with him. "We can see what he cannot, but we cannot make him see unless we first see with him."[1] And to be able to convey a thought or idea in a way likely to be convincing requires that what she wishes to say is sufficiently clear to the worker to allow it to be expressed quite simply and without unnecessary elaboration. Unless this is possible it is wise to be silent.

Using the Transference

Consideration of ways of offering insight brings to the fore the subject of the unconscious meaning that may attach to the material discussed by clients, a subject to which reference has already been made. It is easy for the attention to be engrossed by the literal meaning of ordinary everyday matters that a client may raise, to the disregard both of the reasons that may have brought these to mind, and of their possible unconscious significance in relation to his difficulties. To catch the inner meaning of what is being said requires not only careful listening, as already advocated, but also the thoughtful open-mindedness implied by the question, "In view of all that I know about this client, what may it be that at the moment he is really telling me?" And, in so far as the answer becomes

[1] FREEMAN SHARPE, ELLA. *Collected Papers in Psycho-Analysis*, Chapter 2. London: Hogarth Press, 1950.

clear and if it seems wise and timely to make an interpretation, it is often useful to invite a client's thoughtful participation in some such terms as, "Let us both look at what you have been saying, so that we may be able to see perhaps what it may be telling us and what we may learn from it." Interest in the material that clients spontaneously discuss must never divert attention, however, from the feelings and attitudes that come into activity in the "here and now" of a relationship. This ever-present factor in person-to-person contacts was considered in the last chapter. The matter now at issue is how these dynamic forces of feeling may be met as they arise in casework settings and how, when occasion offers, their nature and origin may be helpfully revealed to clients. The following description of part of a first interview in which transferences of feeling were very clearly revealed will be used to show how they were put to fruitful use:

A mother who had been urged to seek the help of a child guidance clinic, because her son aged twelve was becoming very difficult to manage, was extremely aggressive and uneasy on arrival. She immediately asked the receptionist whether she was likely to be kept waiting and was manifestly uncompromising in attitude when the worker invited her to her room. During the first part of the interview the mother sat stiffly in her chair, showing her irritation by her twitching fingers and forbidding expression. It was obvious to the worker that if real contact was to be made with this very hostile woman she would have to bring these feelings into the open, for otherwise they would stand as a barrier between them. So the worker said that she thought the mother was finding it very difficult to come to the clinic and that she seemed in fact to resent doing so. The mother responded by saying that she was "sick and tired of being asked about my boy's behaviour", which she said she had already discussed with a clergyman and one or two other people; it was they who had urged her to come to the clinic and she added that everyone, including her husband, seemed to think she was to blame for the boy's behaviour and this was not fair.

The worker went on to say that she thought the mother was now thinking that the worker would be likely to take the same view; the mother replied that, speaking truthfully, this was just what she had been thinking before coming to the clinic, but she hadn't liked to refuse to come for fear of blame. She also complained that many people who don't really know much about children were always ready to give advice to mothers "and that made me mad". The worker said at this point, "Well here's another person and an un-married woman at that who you are thinking perhaps is likely to do the same"; a bleak smile then crossed the mother's face and her attitude became slightly more relaxed. The worker then remarked that, as she saw it, the purpose of the mother's visit was to talk about the diffi-culties she was having with her son, with the idea of seeing whether the clinic could be of help and that it was up to her to decide whether or not she wished to use its services; for no one at the clinic wanted to try to help her against her will.

By this time the mother appeared to be less tense and unyielding. Of her own accord she began to talk about herself in a way that revealed some of the reasons under-lying her hostility. She said, for instance, that her own mother had made her feel from childhood onwards that she was a pretty useless person; she was now living nearby and was constantly giving advice on household matters and on the management of the children. To add to her troubles, her mother, like her husband, thought that she was "too easy" with the children, particularly with her son,

F   69

so when her husband had said that it might be a good idea to go to the clinic this had made her feel he had no confidence in her ability to manage her boy. This was really why she had not wished to come. She added that she hadn't dared to refuse because if the boy got into trouble with the police, as she sometimes feared he might because he was mixing with bad boys, she was sure she would be blamed for not having tried to help. By this time tears were not far away. Realizing this and sensing the mother's deep distress about her son, which up to this point she had been unable to admit, the worker said very gently that, although the mother had resented coming to the clinic for the reasons given, wasn't there a bit of herself that was wanting help because she was so worried? The mother nodded in reply.

The worker then brought together some of the mother's comments about her critics, relating them to herself by saying, "I think we can see now why you so hated to come here, for it seems you thought that I, like the people you have mentioned, would criticize and blame you; but I am not wanting to do that; I am anxious to understand what has gone wrong, so that together we may try to find some way of helping you and your son." That this quite simple interpretation of the mother's immediate feelings brought relief was shown by a marked lessening of her hostility and a readiness to enter into a realistic discussion of her boy's behaviour. She was also able to unburden herself of other matters that were causing her anxiety—a not unexpected result when channels of communication are freed.

This case illustrates several points: the helpfulness, for instance, of acknowledging existing feelings whatever their nature, so that the client realizes that they are recognized and accepted without fear and anxiety. It underlines too the importance of interpreting feelings, whether expressed by

70

word or deed, at the moment when they are actually being experienced by the client; to use a colloquialism, when they are "hot". This is exemplified in the worker's comment concerning advice givers, when it became clear that the mother was regarding the worker as yet another of these. Through this interpretative comment the worker was divesting herself of the role in which she was being cast and revealing herself as a person who, contrary to the mother's expectation, was anxious to understand her difficulties rather than to criticize or blame her. Having gained confidence in the worker's good intentions towards her, it then became possible for the mother to discuss her problems frankly and freely.

The Positive Transference

While this example describes the way in which feelings of hostility were brought into the open, relationships will inevitably become the arena in which feelings of every kind will be played out. Some workers find it easier in casework situations to meet hostile feelings than those that are warm and loving, fear of such feelings even making it difficult at times to accept with becoming grace a client's spontaneous expressions of gratitude for help received. The same sense of embarrassment may be experienced if, in the course of a relationship, she becomes for a time, as described earlier in this chapter, the focus of a client's positive feelings, which perhaps have been denied an outlet because of emotional deprivations in the past. Yet it may be a valuable experience for a client to be able to form a relationship in which feelings of affection towards the worker can be simply and naturally expressed without fear of rebuttal. And, if when this happens the worker feels embarrassed, may this be due perhaps to a failure to appreciate the transference significance of these feelings, so that a client's warmth or tendency to over-estimate her qualities is taken personally and at face value?

71

Or may the embarrassment be the result of a failure on the worker's part to come to terms with her own counter-transferences, so that she feels either unduly warm or unduly hostile towards a client? Or may it be that a client's positive feelings are difficult to accept because, deeply within herself, the worker feels that so high a valuation of herself is not really merited? These possibilities, as pointed out in the last chapter, always need to be considered when personal feelings, of whatever nature, tend to obtrude in the course of a case-work relationship.

The value to a client of an opportunity to experience warm feelings towards a worker is shown in the following example:

The client, a somewhat austere and reserved woman in her thirties, was troubled by feelings of indifference towards her husband, a blind man who was extremely demanding of his wife's attentions and jealous of the time she spent in the care of their two young children. The wife, who had known her husband long before marriage was contemplated and before he received a war injury that damaged his sight, had felt impelled to marry him when he asked her to do so after his discharge from the Army, despite his disability and although they both knew that he would ultimately become blind. Whereas she has always been much attached to her father, her relationship with her mother had been far from satisfying; this woman, who was described as "very managing", had given her two daughters good physical care but little real warmth, and the relationships within the whole family were far from satisfactory. It was not surprising that with this background the client was prepared to accept marriage without any deep affection for her husband, her feelings towards him being largely based on pity and a sense of obligation due to their long acquaintanceship, of which she was constantly reminded by her mother. At the time when this girl first came to the agency, her marriage was in a precarious state, for the husband, now totally blind, had become resentful of his helplessness and dependency on her. It seemed evident from her description of the situation that her husband was somewhat suspicious of her, thinking that despite the care and attention she gave him she must be irked by the limitations that his blindness imposed upon their life together and fearing too, though without any grounds, that she might become interested in someone else. The wife had sought the agency's help with her husband's agreement. He also welcomed a visit from the worker, to whom he frankly admitted the difficulties that both were experiencing; in fact, had time and opportunity allowed, it would probably have been advantageous for both partners to have had joint sessions with the worker, so that they could have discussed their difficulties together. But this was precluded by the husband's work, a sheltered trade for which he had been specially trained. He readily agreed, however, to his wife's weekly attendance at the agency, which continued over a period of many months, in the course of which she revealed her anxieties over her inability to give her children the affection she realized they needed.

What appeared most of all to help this emotionally deprived woman during this time was the opportunity the relationship offered for the development of feelings of warmth towards the worker, who became for her the kind and responsive "mother" for whom, as she came to realize, she had always so greatly longed. The transference significance of these feelings was frequently interpreted to her as the work continued. And though for a time the client depended very greatly on the worker, tending to over-estimate her qualities and capacities for understanding, the relationship, having brought to life dormant capacities for gentleness and affection, was then the means through which she became able to bring the fruit of this experience into her relationships with her husband and children. Having as it were been warmed herself, she was then able to warm others. As might be expected, this change of attitude did not come about quickly or without difficulty. It was not easy, for instance, for this woman to accept the limitations of a professional relationship, wanting it to become one that was personal and social in character. It was also difficult for her to acknowledge, either to herself or the worker, the negative feelings sometimes provoked by the denial of these wishes, fearing that they would damage a relationship on which she set much store. These matters had to be brought into the open, so that she could come to see that although her wishes could not be satisfied, the worker's interest in her would continue as a source of helpfulness upon which she could draw.

Now it would have been easy for the worker to have allowed these feelings to gain strength, and perhaps to have become so enveloping that this emotionally deprived woman would virtually have lost sight of the worker as a real person and have come to see her idealistically. Such over-valuation of another human being in a casework relationship would not have helped her to cope with her situation and, therefore, an important aim was to enable her to view the worker realistically. For this purpose an attempt was made to bring together the client's conscious memories and fantasies of a rejecting mother, which she had so often expressed, doing so at moments when associated feelings and attitudes were very much alive and being projected onto the worker; at the same time her attention was drawn to her over-valuation of the worker and to the probability that this was the outcome of a desire to find in the latter the good and loving mother of her dreams. It may be useful here to mention the different way in

74

which the client's feelings towards the worker would have been dealt with were she in analysis. The aim of the work would then have been to enable the patient to regress emotionally in the relationship with the analyst, who for the time being would represent a parent. Thus the unconscious and conscious loves and hates of infancy and childhood would be given an opportunity of being re-lived in their intensity and depth; so that they could gradually become relinquished in favour of more mature feelings and attitudes as they were played out, interpreted, and worked through in the course of the analysis.

Extra-Transference Interpretations

As well as offering insight through the interpretation of feelings transferred from a past relationship to a present one, it is often helpful when working with a client to draw his attention to the fact that feelings formerly attaching to some situation or circumstance in the past are revived by subsequent situations and experiences with which they are associatively linked. An example may be helpful in clarifying this point:

A young mother, when discussing her difficulties in caring for her two young children, complained among other things of the annoyance caused her by her elder daughter, aged five, who was always following her about while she was trying to do her housework. The mother said that she had not much experience of children, having had only one sister eight years younger than herself. She remarked that other mothers had told her that their children often did this sort of thing and that they seemed able to tolerate it, but to her it was "maddening". She admitted to feelings of shame over this, but justified herself on the score that it was impossible to run her home properly unless she worked

75

to a routine and this she could not do with a child always at her heels. Asked by the worker about her early life, she said that even as a little girl she had always liked to plan her day and had often got into a lot of trouble with her own mother, who used to tell her she was selfish because she didn't want to interrupt her play in order to amuse her little sister. The analogy between the two situations described was striking, so much so that the worker was not surprised when the mother paused, "as though the penny had dropped"; in fact she laughed aloud when the worker remarked that the mother's annoying little daughter seemed to bear a very close resemblance to the annoying little sister of bygone days. It then seemed that a mirror, having as it were been placed before her, she was able to see for herself what it revealed.

It would be unwise to over-estimate the usefulness to clients of helping them to relate like to like as described above, for in some instances, to do so might lead solely to an intellectual appreciation of similarities, which, while interesting, would be ineffective in modifying attitudes or behaviour. But in this instance the client developed genuine insight, realizing that in some ways she was feeling towards her child less like a grown-up mother and more like a petulant and jealous older sister. In consequence life became a little easier for her child, who up to now had had to bear the brunt not only of feelings aroused in her mother by her own behaviour, but also of those that sprang from an earlier source.

Timing Interpretations
It is by no means easy to judge the moment to bring out a truth so that its acceptance is likely, or to be deft and skilful in so doing. The importance of making a transference interpretation at the time when the feelings to which it is directed

are uppermost has already been pointed out, for it is then that there is likely to be response, because the moment is one of dawning conviction. This holds true for any interpretative comments that are made, for unless they link in with feelings that are actually being experienced, they will fall on stony ground. Of course, however apt an interpretation may seem to be, the truth that it holds may be resisted or denied, perhaps because it has been offered prematurely or because it is too unwelcome to be readily accepted. But sometimes, even when resistance and denial are met, a seed may have been sown that will bear fruit later. There will be occasions, however, when to offer insight would be both useless and unwise, a case in point being the one described in the last chapter in respect of the man whose attention was attracted to a damaged building on his way to the agency. While this client revealed much regarding his underlying emotional difficulties, which helped the worker to assess the situation, to have interpreted to him the unconscious significance of his comments at the time they were made would have been fruitless, since the strength of his defences, as shown by his general attitude and projections, made it likely that incredulity and denial would have been the only outcome. Further work with this man soon proved that his problems were beyond the reach of casework help; for, while he was ready enough to point out the need for members of his family to alter their ways, he saw no reason whatsoever for changes to take place in himself.

Need for Diagnostic Appraisal

This last instance provides a reminder, if such is needed, of the limitations of casework, a matter that, in the interests of clients, must always be frankly faced. For, apart from lack of insight and skill on the worker's part, which may restrict her usefulness to people in trouble, there will be many occasions when the presence of deep-seated emotional difficulties or firmly fixed character disorders in the client will make it impossible for problems to be dealt with through the means available to caseworkers. Some clients who ask for help will be quite unprepared to spend the time and effort required, and others will withdraw if faced with truths that are unacceptable. It is often difficult to judge the nature and extent of a problem when a client is seen initially, but experience has shown that much time and effort is sometimes expended on work ultimately proved fruitless, because no attempt was made at an early stage to estimate the sincerity of the client's desire for help and his willingness and capacity to cooperate, or to try to assess a problem in respect both of its suitability for casework help and the worker's ability to give it. The following brief account of work that came to a premature end provides an example of wasted effort which was largely due to failure to give careful thought to these matters before help was offered:

The mother of a boy of twelve was urged by the family doctor to bring him to a child guidance clinic because of difficulty in getting him to go to school. On her first visit she said that his ill health had often prevented him from attending and that for several months he had not gone at all, fearing that he would be sick if he did so. She admitted, however, that her doctor had said there were no medical grounds for absence, for the boy's bronchial trouble, at one time persistent, had now cleared up. When he attended the clinic he was found to be very small for his age, a frail looking, immature child of odd appearance who seemed extremely dependent on his mother. The psychologist found him to be of good intelligence and surprisingly well informed, despite his infrequent school attendance. It was also learned that, although his mother thought him so

78

delicate, he often took quite long bicycle rides into the country. Apart from this he had few interests and shunned the company of other boys. In the initial talks with his mother it became clear that a strong emotional tie existed between herself and her son. He was her youngest child and only boy and, as she frankly admitted, he meant more to her than any of her other four children, his delicacy from infancy upwards (probably more fancied than real) apparently making an irresistible appeal to her maternal feelings.

When enlarging upon her own life prior to her marriage, it became evident that she had grown up in a harsh environment in which the absence of warm and loving relationships had led her to expect little happiness from life. She had married her husband against the wishes of her parents, who disliked him and warned her that all he wanted was a home and someone to look after him. She was sure, however, that life with him would be pleasanter than life at home, where, apparently without protest, she had continually been imposed upon and belittled. But her parents' words came true, for she soon found her husband to be extremely selfish, demanding, and contemptuous of her, as the worker realized when she met him. It was not surprising, therefore, that throughout her married life she had turned to her children for the satisfaction of emotional needs denied her by her husband, or that in her son's delicacy she had found justification for the doting care she had always given him from infancy upwards. It seemed likely indeed, as the mother described her difficulties in getting her son to school, that, despite her outward anxieties on this score, the strength of the emotional tie between them was making it difficult, if not impossible, for either of them to accept the separation that school attendances necessitated. Nevertheless, with misleading zeal she accepted

79

the offer of weekly psychotherapy for her son and regular discussions of her problem with the worker. But after two successive weekly attendances mother and son came at widely spaced intervals and ceased to do so altogether after six visits. The mother wrote meanwhile giving fatigue or illness as a reason for their absences, reasons to which she held with tenacity when seen by chance on one occasion.

This is a case in which mother and son were firmly welded together in a bond that neither wished to sever, because of the mutual satisfaction it gave them. As far as this boy's emotional life was concerned, to all intents and purposes he was at the level of a toddler; for although he occasionally showed some signs of physical independence, through his bicycle rides and a few other activities, like the very young child he always returned pretty quickly to the shelter of the maternal wing, the mother's emotional deprivations making her only too ready to welcome him back; in fact each unconsciously encouraged and supported the other's neurosis. It seems likely that this boy will continue to be successful in evading attempts, legal or otherwise, to get him regularly to school, because his pathetic appearance, his ready escape into illness at times of pressure, reinforced by his mother's support, will always stand him in good stead. The mother's need for the emotional outlet provided by her son's dependency also suggests that had some means been found of emancipating him, her own precarious mental state might have worsened. And could he himself bear the strain either of physical or emotional separation from her? This seems unlikely.

The particular approach to clients and their problems that has been advocated in these pages may not appeal to every caseworker. It is a desciplined approach, and therefore requires study and thought, and, as pointed out in the first chapter, a true assimilation of the psychological concepts on which it is based if it is to be used effectively. For these reasons the ideas that have been put forward may be questioned by those who prefer to work empirically. It is hoped, however, that those who find themselves in accord, either wholly or in part, with the formulation of theory and practice that has been attempted may find it both helpful and enriching to their work.

PART II
CASE STUDIES

CHAPTER 5

Casework with an Adoptive Parent in a Single Interview

Mrs. A came to see a caseworker at an agency for one brief interview, ostensibly to discuss whether she and her husband should inform their son, aged five years, that he was adopted. She had written beforehand to ask for an appointment, but had given no indication in her letter of what the problem was. On arrival she gave the impression of being a forthright business-like person. She at once thanked the worker for giving her an appointment, said she hoped she wasn't being a bother in taking up her time, and then proceeded at once to tell her story in a direct and unemotional way. Mrs A said that unfortunately she was unable to have children. This had been a very serious disappointment to herself and her husband, since they had always hoped to have a family. They were now very glad that they had taken the step of adopting a child, for the boy, whom they had had since he was a year old, had brought them great happiness. No one except their relatives and a few close friends knew that their child was adopted, since they had moved several times during the past five years.

Mrs. A said both she and her husband had thought a good deal about the age at which the child should be told of his adoption, and were now feeling that perhaps this should be delayed no longer. She alluded to a talk on the wireless that they had recently heard, to the effect that it was unwise to keep adopted children in ignorance of the facts of their birth. She discussed this at some length, adding that what she really feared was that if the truth were known when the child went to school, other children, and even adults, might "take it out of him". She remarked that adopted children were often looked down on even by grown-up people who ought to know better, adding "and that makes it hard for people like me who can't have children." Mrs. A laid so much stress on the anticipated attitude of others towards her son that the worker wondered whether she herself had entirely accepted him. Was she perhaps projecting on to others feelings that to some extent she shared? The worker therefore asked Mrs A to tell her how the child fitted into their home. Mrs. A then enlarged on the happiness he had brought both to her husband and to herself, saying what a lovable, happy little chap he was and how he had helped to fill the blank in their lives, consequent upon her misfortune. She also said how much she had suffered when she learned she could never bear children.

At this point the worker hazarded the suggestion that perhaps, in discussing how people might feel if they knew about the adoption, Mrs. A was expressing a fear that people might despise her too for her inability to have children. Mrs. A looked at the worker reflectively and said, "Well, perhaps you are right, because I have never wanted people to know that the boy isn't my own," adding, "Somehow or other I always feel so ashamed that I can't have children and perhaps that is why I find it difficult to tell the boy that he is not my own child." The worker agreed that this might be so and said,

"Would you like to tell me more about your feelings of unhappiness on this score?" With considerable emotion, but also with evident relief, Mrs. A then spoke of her childlessness, adding that this was particularly difficult for her because her three sisters had children of their own and she often felt jealous and unhappy when she visited them. She often wondered too whether they looked down on her; the worker then remarked that perhaps Mrs A might be thinking that she, the worker, also shared her sisters' feelings. This was laughingly denied, but Mrs A went on to say that it was pleasant to talk things over with someone who seemed to understand her difficulties. She again talked at some length about the happiness that their boy had brought to her husband and herself and described their plans for his education. She repeated that she was sure they should tell him about his adoption as soon as possible. The worker agreed that their decision was a wise one. Mrs. A thanked the worker for having seen her and seemed pleased when the worker said that she would be very glad to see Mrs A again should she need her help at any time.

Comment

There are several points arising from this interview that justify further discussion. It seemed clear from the way it developed that, although Mrs. A gave one reason for coming to the agency, either consciously or unconsciously she had another aim in mind. It was evident from the start that both she and her husband had made up their minds to tell the child of his adoption and needed no advice on this score. In fact this subject soon faded into the background. This case therefore provides a useful illustration of the fact that so often the presenting problem is less important to the client than others he has in mind.

It has been seen too that Mrs. A had much to say concerning the possible attitude of others towards her son. Although it may sometimes happen that adopted children are subject to unkindness on this account, Mrs. A's anxieties seemed excessive, leading the worker to suppose or suspect that she was projecting on to the outside world feelings that to some extent were her own. When a client seems to be projecting, a worker may sometimes be tempted to jump to conclusions and to share her understanding with the client before she is clear that he is ready to accept it. It seemed, for instance, that Mrs. A was unaware of any negative feelings towards her son, and would merely have been distressed or antagonized by any suggestion that they existed. It is often extremely difficult, as has been stressed in the text, to know when insight can usefully be given. Whereas the presence of certain feelings may seem clear enough to the worker, skill lies in knowing whether to bring them into the open, or, as in this instance, to refrain. All that the worker sought to do at this point was to suggest that Mrs. A should tell her more about the family relationships, thus trying to elicit further information and discover whether the suspected feelings were near the threshold of conscious thought. The question was put in a general way; it was in fact an "open-ended" question, that is to say one that is unweighted by the worker's impressions, in contrast to one that anticipates the presence of a particular feeling, such as, "I think perhaps you may be feeling. . . ." The worker's question brought forth eulogistic comments concerning the happiness that the child had brought to his adoptive parents, suggesting that whatever the underlying feelings might be, on a conscious level the situation was a happy one, which should be left undisturbed. It seemed, however, that Mrs A wanted to uncover her unhappiness about her childlessness and her fear, so frankly discussed, of being despised because of it. Her remarks concerning other people's possible attitudes to her boy appeared in fact to contain a hint of her fear of rejection by others on this score, and perhaps as well a hint of her own self-criticism. The worker's intervention appropriately touched anxieties that were evidently in the forefront of her mind. At this point the worker included herself with those who might be critical of Mrs. A, believing that Mrs. A felt her to be so. This was in accordance with the principle that feelings and thoughts ascribed by a client to others usually refer in some measure to the person to whom such comments are made. Although by implication Mrs A appeared to set aside the worker's comment, this by no means indicated its rejection. In fact, her subsequent remark concerning the worker's sympathetic understanding suggested that it had been both comforting and reassuring.

CHAPTER 6

Casework with a Client
in a Financial Difficulty

Mr. B came to a social agency on his own initiative to ask for a loan of £70 to pay for some goods he required for his business. He said that he had recently acquired a small general store which he found needed more alteration and modernization than he had anticipated, with the result that he was now short of ready money to pay for the necessary re-stocking, and pressure was being put on him by one of his wholesalers to pay a bill that had been owing for some months. Mr. B said he had been intensely worried about this and was wondering to whom he could turn when he happened to pass the agency's office and suddenly thought that perhaps someone there might be able to help him. He said, very apologetically, that he had never asked for help from anyone before, and was evidently extremely embarrassed at doing so and afraid he might be asking too much.

The worker asked Mr. B to tell her as much as he could about his business affairs, so that together they could think through the situation and discover perhaps what might be done. Mr. B said that he had been employed since boyhood as a grocer's assistant and had steadily saved throughout the years with the idea of setting up in a business of his own. He had recently received a small legacy from a relative, and had thought that this and his savings provided enough capital to establish himself, thus fulfilling his life's ambition. He said he was the youngest of the family and had two older brothers, both of whom now owned grocery businesses. He felt that he could not ask them for help because he did not want them to know that he was in a difficulty, adding that the worker must think he had been "a bit of a fool" to have got himself into this mess. The worker said she realized that he was very uneasy at asking for a loan and it seemed as if he, more than anyone else, was thinking he was "a bit of a fool" and that was why perhaps he felt that everyone, including herself, would undoubtedly think the same. Mr. B seemed encouraged by this comment. He then told her that he had never been as successful in life as his two brothers. They had done much better in school and had always "gone ahead" and now were much better off than himself. He added, "They have not much use for me; I am the dud of the family."

It seemed evident from all this that setting up in business held considerable emotional significance for Mr. B, as suggested by his comments about his brother's superior abilities and his apparent desire to emulate them. With this in mind, the worker asked him once again to tell her about his financial difficulties. Mr. B said he had been a little more extravagant over the redecoration of his shop than perhaps he should have been and described his attempts to make it more convenient and attractive. Although he had said he had come to the agency by chance, he now produced various documents relating to the transfer of the business and the expenses he had incurred, so that he and the worker were able to consider them together. The details of expenditure certainly suggested somewhat lavish spending in relation to the apparently modest nature of the business. The worker commented on this, remarking that perhaps in setting up his shop so well he had some idea in his mind that it must come up to the standards of his brothers. He admitted quite frankly that this was so, remarking that he did not want them to think when they saw it that he had landed himself with a "pig in a poke", but now it looked as though they would have the laugh on him when they knew of his present difficulties. The worker said that perhaps he was thinking she too might have similar thoughts to his brothers'. He repeated that he certainly had found it hard to talk about his difficulties, because he felt he should not have got himself into his present predicament. The worker said that a loan could not be considered unless there was a reasonable chance of the business succeeding, and anyway agency funds were limited. She wanted Mr. B fully to understand this and she was sure that being a business man himself he would be able to appreciate the agency's point of view. He agreed that this was reasonable enough and suggested that the worker should visit him to "have a look round". This she promised to do. Mr. B then said good-bye, apparently less tense and unhappy than he had been on arrival.

Comment

This case, like the previous one, illustrates the importance of bringing into the open transferred feelings that a client is experiencing. Had the worker neglected to relate herself to the embarrassment Mr. B was feeling when meeting her, he would probably have continued throughout the interview to be at the mercy of it. By communicating to him her awareness of his feelings, she was in effect saying to him, "I am not the critical person you expect me to be, but rather someone who is prepared to listen sympathetically, with the object of finding ways and means of helping you." That the worker had sensed Mr. B's feelings correctly was indicated by his subsequent remarks, which showed that she had been representing to him, in the transference, the brothers and perhaps others who had "never thought much of me", a concept of her that might have adversely affected the relationship had she failed to bring it into the open.

It is quite obvious that a simple comment of this kind, however insightful and accurate it may be, cannot dispose of feelings that are the outcome of a life-time's experience. It seems very likely, for instance, that this man had always suffered from feelings of inferiority and emotional insecurity. None the less, the worker's comment appeared to encourage him, perhaps because he saw that she had perceived his difficulties but was not prejudiced by what he had told her of his failings or the alleged opinions of others about him. It seemed obvious from this interview that this man's relationship with his brothers had considerable bearing on his present predicament, for he seemed to be still in active rivalry with them; hence the worker's comment showing him that she recognized the existence of these feelings and was aware of their influence on the way he conducted his business affairs. It is also worth noting that, when the worker drew his attention to the agency's point of view over the matter of the loan, she was then making a first move towards bringing this man into partnership with herself. It is always important, as has been seen, to try to mobilize the capacities of clients for intelligent participation in the discussion of their affairs, thus stimulating potentials for self-help and self-direction.

CHAPTER 7

Casework with a Patient in a Hospital Ward

This is an account of a brief contact with a patient in a hospital ward.

Miss C, aged 55 years, was admitted to hospital for cardiac investigation and proved to have fairly severe mitral stenosis. She was a tall, thin, rather prematurely aged person. She came from a district well outside the area served by the hospital and because of this did not receive visitors quite as often as most patients in the ward.

No formal social history was taken either by the almoner or the medical staff, but the following facts emerged gradually during three short interviews.

Miss C was the eldest child of a family of four—the first three children (i.e. Miss C, a brother, and then a sister) were born within the space of three years, and the youngest child, a boy, was born eight years after Miss C. The family had been in poor circumstances, particularly during the early years of the parents' marriage. The father's earnings were low and the mother had to supplement the income by taking in washing. Miss C had had chorea in childhood and at least

94

one period of hospital treatment; this illness had left her with a heart lesion, although it was not clear whether this had been fully appreciated at the time. She had worked for the same firm of furriers ever since she was twenty, working her way up to a position as workroom supervisor. She had remained single and always lived with her parents; the other children had married, but her sister and brother-in-law had lived in the same house for many years. Her mother and father had died within the four years preceding Miss C's admission to hospital. Mother died first and then father was ill and was nursed at home for a long time before his death. He was said to have had fits, although the nature of these fits and how long he had been subject to them was not specified. Following this Miss C had found it an increasing strain to manage her work and was on the verge of collapse when admitted to hospital.

INTERVIEW I

When Miss C had been in the ward three weeks the almoner, who had been talking to another patient and was about to leave the ward, noticed Miss C making signs indicating that she wished to speak to her. She had made a reasonable recovery and was sitting out of bed. She consulted the almoner about various insurance and sickness benefit claims she needed to make, bringing out a sheaf of correspondence with considerable agitation. She spoke rapidly and at first incoherently, but after listening quietly for some time it was clear to the almoner that Miss C was not only intelligent enough to deal with these practical matters herself, but that she had set the wheels in motion competently already. Miss C said she thought she had understood about it, but wanted to make sure it was all right. She continued to look very anxious and seemed scarcely able to sit still, and while she talked about the insurances she also stressed the fact that she was at a distance from her home. The almoner asked if this was making her feel unsettled; Miss C said that she did feel very unsettled and worried about her treatment and what the outcome would be, but she was afraid to approach the doctor, "who might think that I am asking for special attention".

The almoner said perhaps she and Miss C could discuss this difficulty, although she could not stay with her just then as lunch was about to be served; perhaps Miss C would like her to come up at a more convenient time when there would be an opportunity for a longer talk. Miss C agreed, although she still seemed tense and restless.

Comment

This patient had not been referred to the almoner by the medical or nursing staff, although she had been in the ward for three weeks and one would suppose that she had been agitated for some time. There are two possible explanations for this. First, her excessive fussiness and excitability no doubt affected those about her in a rather unnerving way— in fact the almoner, suddenly confronted with the patient's agitated and precipitate advances, had to deal firmly with her own reactions, especially as at that moment her mind was full of a pressing and difficult problem of the patient she had just left. Second, the patient herself seemed unable to voice her feelings effectively to the doctor, partly because she was so muddled about her problem that she did not feel a busy doctor could give her the time her problems demanded and she was uncertain what his attitude would be.

During her treatment in the ward, Miss C must have seen the almoner with other patients on several occasions, and she seems to have taken some time to decide whether or not to approach her. Eventually she asked advice about a practical matter, which it was soon evident she could handle herself. Perhaps this is not unusual—many clients seem to displace their agitation about an emotional problem that they only dimly perceive, on to a problem they can put into words; or they may ask advice about something it is quite safe to mention when they are not sure whether the real trouble will be understood and accepted, and it is the job of the worker to sense this and try to understand what the underlying problem is. In this case it seemed that seeking advice on a practical matter was not Miss C's main or fundamental objective, but that she was extremely guilty about her need for help and afraid that if she asked for it she would be thought excessively demanding or rejected as a nuisance. She was almost certainly saying at first, "Are you going to notice my anxiety and is it all right to be anxious?", and then, "Are you going to understand what my anxiety is about?"

In this very short interview the almoner conveyed to Miss C her recognition of the anxiety and, by noticing how she expressed her problem, was able to link it up with her illness and admission to hospital and the situation in which Miss C now found herself.

It would probably have been helpful to have continued the interview, but for several reasons this was not done:

1. Ward routine threatened to interrupt a longer talk.

2. The almoner's own reaction to the patient's agitation had to be dealt with.

3. The degree of agitation suggested that Miss C's problems were probably severe and raised the question of how far one could go in helping her. The almoner also had to consider how much time could be given to Miss C in view of the needs of other patients.

4. The fact that she was already up and nearing discharge to an address well outside the usual area meant that regular interviews after discharge would be impossible and this had to be borne in mind.

97

Before this interview the physician had recommended a period of convalescence and the almoner had been asked to make the arrangements.

Conversation about the proposed convalescence soon led into Miss C's difficulties; she expressed concern about her condition, saying she had been examined by the cardiologist two days ago but "he had said nothing." . . . "All I want to know is if I am fit to go back to work." The almoner encouraged her to talk about her work. Miss C said that she had worked for her firm for thirty-five years and had continued in her job after the family removed further away. This meant that she had to get up at 5.00 a.m. every morning and did not arrive home until 7.00 p.m. She had worked her way up steadily to workroom supervisor and was on her feet all day long; she found the responsibility rather a strain, although she had hoped to remain with the firm until she was sixty and qualified for a pension. She had a long hill to climb every morning, which she had felt increasingly unable to face, and when she got home at night she did her share of the housework in spite of her fatigue. The almoner here asked if it would not be possible to have some help in the house if the married sister also went out to work. Miss C said that if she gave up work she would not be able "to pay my share" at home, and the sister "will not allow me to have domestic help." This led to talk about the family situation.

It will be remembered that Miss C had lost both parents within the last four years, that her mother died first and that her father, who had been considerably older, had been ill for a long time at home and had had fits and been violent at times. Miss C had to cope with all this. Her married sister had stayed at home and looked after him during the day, but

98

Miss C had nursed him at night although she had been at work all day. She said that her sister had not expected her to do the night nursing, but she added quickly that anyway *she* had felt she *had* to do this for her parents.

When her father died Miss C had thought of giving up work and letting rooms in the home, but the sister had "just asked for extra rooms" for herself and her husband and Miss C "could not refuse her". Miss C said that she did anything to keep the peace and could not risk unpleasantness. The sister now went out to work again, but still only continued to pay half the expenses although she had the extra rooms and her husband was working. Miss C brought out all this in a hesitant, veiled manner, but the almoner sensed extreme jealousy and aggression coupled with guilt behind it all and drew Miss C's attention to this possibility.

Miss C denied that she was jealous and went on to say that her sister had "always been the spoilt baby"—mother had had three pregnancies in less than three years, Miss C being the eldest, then a brother with whom she had very little contact now, and then the married sister. Miss C followed this by saying that she herself had therefore "never been able to be a child". Father had been a carpenter, "was slow all his life", and money had been very short, so mother had taken in washing, "but for this she had received a mere pittance". Miss C said that there had been no workers to help in those days and "all this had gone on behind closed doors". The almoner suggested that this must have put a great burden on the children. Miss C agreed, but said how good her mother had been to them all and how difficult it had been for mother when they were very young. The almoner said it sounded as though it had been difficult for them all, but as Miss C was the eldest child perhaps she had felt things most acutely. One could not blame her if she had felt hurt and resentful at being supplanted so early in the affections of her parents by two younger siblings, nor as a young child being jealous of mother's concern for father and giving so much of her time to her work. In fact Miss C had hinted at this in saying that she had "never been able to be a child". She now said that *she* had been the one who helped mother most, in fact would do anything for her. The almoner suggested that perhaps working hard had been one way in which Miss C reassured herself that mother still needed her and that she herself loved mother—in a way she had had to work hard to keep her parents' love and now, even today, it was almost as though she felt compelled to go on working harder than she need.

Although Miss C made no direct comment, her manner had been growing less tense and her next remarks suggested that she had been able to accept something at least of the idea that her earlier experiences could have some bearing on her present inability to relax, both in regard to her job and in the house.

She went on to say that she was feeling much better since her admission to hospital and was really quite frightened of her present desire and ability to relax and let things go. The almoner discussed her ambivalence about this a little—the drive to exert herself and remain independent, and her need to relax and come to some compromise with the situation. Miss C then revealed that she had been turning over alternative plans, wondering whether, if she remained at home and looked after the house, her sister and brother-in-law would pay a larger proportion of the rent, but she still felt unable to ask them. She said that her younger brother was born eight years after her, "when times were easier"; he was the one who understood her and talked things over with her. She had evidently talked with him quite recently about giving up work, for he had queried whether she could apply for National Assistance since she had about £400 saved.

She then reverted to her work and the pension scheme in

100

which she had some money. Her employer had put off organizing the scheme for years, although he ought to have done so long ago. It had not long been started and she did not know exactly what her position would be if she gave up work, or if she came to some agreement to work shorter hours; but again she felt she could not ask about this. She thought that her brother could do so, but so far she had not asked him. The almoner said that if she gave up work she should apply to the National Assistance Board, which disregarded capital up to a certain amount, but their decision would rest on their estimate of her total resources.

Miss C evidently found it most difficult to talk knowledgeably about the financial situation and was anxious that all this should be treated as confidential, especially in relation to the doctors, for fear that they should feel she was pleading poverty. She repeated again, "I only want to know if doctor thinks I can go back to work." The almoner pointed out that in order to advise her the doctor must know a little of the situation, but perhaps she might like the almoner to have a talk with him. She agreed to this arrangement, it seemed with some relief.

Towards the end of the interview, Miss C talked more about her mother, how much she had loved her and how perfect she had been and how glad she was she had done all she could for her. Then she started to ask questions about the almoner's family, asking if her mother was alive still and if she had sisters. The almoner said that perhaps Miss C was wondering if she too had had similar problems in relation to her family and if perhaps, as well as loving them very much, she had sometimes felt angry and disappointed with the parents, and jealous of her sisters, especially as Miss C could see that the almoner was herself unmarried. Miss C did not take this up, but again emphasized her complete satisfaction with her mother and how much she missed her.

H   101

Comment

1. In this interview Miss C was able to speak almost at once about her difficulties, and much more freely than before, and one would suppose that the almoner's previous acceptance of her anxiety had been a help.

2. That the cardiologist had "told me nothing" was not strictly true, since some information is usually given to patients after examination. Her next sentence, "All I want to know is whether I can go back to work or not", indicated that (a) the cardiologist had not told her what she wanted, (b) she could not make any use of what he had said, and (c) she had been unable to explain what was troubling her.

If all she had wanted was an answer to a simple question, it is difficult to understand why she had been unable to ask it; this confirmed the almoner's view that she really had very little insight into the nature of her anxiety and into what going to work or leaving it meant to her. In fact, it was not so much an answer to this question she needed just then, as some clarification of the conflicting emotions underlying it; once more it was not just straightforward advice or information she needed, although she consciously put it in this form. The almoner, perceiving this, encouraged her to talk more freely and it was not long before Miss C referred to the family situation and her relationship to her young married sister.

3. It became clear that (a) she was burdening herself with a journey and hours of work that would have been arduous for a perfectly healthy person, and (b) she appeared to have accepted—almost demanded—the burden of nursing her parents, as if she could not bear to relinquish their care to her sister even though the latter appeared to have given up to help and to enable Miss C to keep her job. Indeed, the fact that her sister was at home and had the parents to herself all

day may have been a factor in Miss C's feeling that she *had* to take on the night duty; it was as if this was a challenge in the competition between the sisters for the love and approbation of the parents (e.g. Miss C's repeated reference to "my share"). This attitude was carried over on to the problem of the housework and the financial arrangements. Miss C pictured the younger sister as greedy, demanding, and inconsiderate, taking more than her share all the time. In talking about all this Miss C appeared anxious rather than angry and the almoner could not help feeling that the anxiety belonged to Miss C's fear of her own greed and her fear of retaliation by her sister and the disapproval and loss of love of her parents. In fact, in the first interview Miss C had expressed her anxiety lest the doctor think she was asking for special attention, but it was now carried a step further back into the family setting. This no doubt was partly due to the almoner's acceptance of the patient's anxiety in the first interview.

4. When it was gently said that perhaps Miss C might sometimes feel jealous of her sister, this was immediately denied. Repudiation of a suggestion need not always imply that it is erroneous and Miss C's next remarks hinted that in this instance the suggestion was correct, so much so that Miss C was able to enlarge on it and explain how this situation had originated and grown.

Her statement that "there were no workers to help in those days, and all this went on behind closed doors" might possibly have indicated uncertainty and guilt about approaching a worker, but it also gave a vivid impression of the family tension, which Miss C had taken very much inside herself; hence the almoner's remark that this must have put a great burden on the children. This immediately led Miss C to speak of her mother's goodness, as if any suggestion of dissatisfaction felt like incitement to criticize her mother.

She seemed to have been left with the permanent feeling that she had not had her share of good things (i.e. of mother and father), and her anger and jealousy had had to be suppressed for fear they would be condemned and bring a further loss of parental love. She may have thought that to work hard was one way of keeping mother's love, and also of dealing with her jealousy of her siblings, since it emphasized her seniority and indispensability. The worker's comment that she had always had to work hard to keep her parents' love was an endeavour to suggest all this, stressing not only her need for affection, but her positive love for her mother and how these feelings were operative in the present. It is sometimes tempting to draw attention to the hostile feelings at the expense of the loving ones, but it is important, and in this case was very important, to acknowledge the patient's loving feelings.

The suggestions that were offered were not profound, but Miss C's reference to closed doors indicated to the almoner that, at a more primitive level, Miss C's difficulties probably referred to her childhood curiosity and fantasies about her parents' intimate relationships, and perhaps to secret thoughts and activities of her own about which she was extremely guilty and for which she feared punishment. Perhaps she was also wondering what the almoner might be concealing from her and whether it was safe to trust her further. Miss C's behaviour and conversation in the third interview provided some confirmation of this, but at the time, bearing in mind that their relationship was probably to be short, the almoner did not feel able to make comments that might have enabled Miss C to reveal deeper feelings, neither did she consider that it would have been particularly helpful for her to do so.

5. Miss C was able sufficiently to accept the almoner's way of putting things to appreciate some of the reasons for her anxiety, including her immediate conflict between wanting

to relax and feeling that she must stand on her own feet. Her underlying need for dependence, however, was so great that she was "afraid of my ability to relax". One could wonder here whether she really wanted to know, "Am I fit to go back to work?", and not rather, "May I give up the struggle without feeling too guilty about it?" By dwelling on her ambivalence, the almoner seemed to help Miss C to see how far she herself had tried to go towards dealing with this problem. Almost immediately she came up against Miss C's inability to approach either her sister or her employer, and her hesitation about asking her brother to act as mediator. It was clear at this point that it might be impossible to achieve much more with Miss C in one interview, and having decided to limit the aim in this case, the almoner obtained her agreement to seeing the doctor.

6. The talk about her employer, who had put off organizing a pension scheme, and her own difficulties in asking about it, might be seen as a projection of Miss C's feelings about the almoner whom she had seen talking to other patients and who had, so to speak, "put off" talking to Miss C, who had only been able to approach her with difficulty and anxiety.

7. Miss C then asked the almoner about her personal life; perhaps because she was identifying herself with the almoner, as someone like herself who did kind things for others. Sometimes this switching of the conversation onto the worker's personal life appears to be a defence against feelings of helplessness when the worker's handling of a situation seems too threatening, as if the patient, feeling threatened, reverses roles with the worker and puts her into the category of patient. Interpretation of the need to question is usually sufficient and direct answers to questions are as a rule best avoided if a professional relationship is to be maintained and if the patient is to be helped to understand her own attitudes.

Miss C was again seen in the ward. She appeared calmer and said the doctor had been to see her and had been so kind to her—"He has spent a whole quarter of an hour with me", whereas before she had not felt he had time for her.

She also said that her brother had been to see the doctor—a development that she seemed to have accepted without resentment—and together they had talked over the doctor's suggestion that she might find a lighter job nearer home, or her brother's suggestion that she might start to take paying guests. She felt this had all been due to talking to the almoner, which had been a great help, "as you cannot talk to everyone, especially your relations".

She then brought out a card issued well over forty years previously by a children's hospital, where she had received in-patient treatment for two months for chorea. The card was addressed to her father, and read something as follows: "You are required to fetch your daughter home on such and such a date at the termination of her treatment." It sounded brusque and dictatorial—it was grey with age and appeared to have been carried in Miss C's bag for a long time. The almoner asked about this experience, and Miss C said that for the first month she had been isolated behind a red screen, strapped down to her bed and allowed no toys. She watched the other children through the screen playing with their toys and had felt her treatment to be a punishment. She said how different methods of treatment were now, but supposed they had really been right and the treatment had done her good. Even when showing the almoner the old card, she had suggested what a nice card it was, as if the message on it had been couched in the most considerate terms. That her relationship with her father was reflected in this story seems obvious, but no comments were made because it was difficult

106

at the time for the almoner to understand what all this was about. She told Miss C how to deal with her National Health Certificates on transfer to the convalescent home and hoped she would have a further opportunity to rest and relax.

Comment

Miss C appeared to have received an answer to her question about going back to work—what precisely she decided to do was left to her and the family to work out. She had at any rate been able to make some use of the doctor's discussion with her, and although she said that this was the first occasion he had given her so much of his time, it could perhaps be claimed that her interviews with the almoner had given her a belief that people might want to help her. It will be remembered that on the first occasion she had been too anxious to be able to take in what the doctor said and to consider it.

It would be interesting to speculate further on the significance of showing the almoner the old hospital card. This, by present day standards, appeared dictatorial, but Miss C suggested that it was all that could be desired. She talked about very distressing experiences in hospital, but said she thought her treatment had been right and had done her good. The almoner could not help being reminded that Miss C had spoken of her parents very much in this vein and wondered if, once more, Miss C was saying, "Look, I feel very badly about these experiences, but I dare not let myself express my feelings unless you will help me with them." It is of interest that the card was addressed to Miss C's father, to whom her references had been noticeably slight. However, the fact that she had preserved it for over forty years and still carried it about with her, indicated what tremendous significance it must have had for her, and perhaps pointed to very strong underlying feelings for her father. It was he, at least, who had taken her out of hospital where she had had unhappy and frightening experiences.

Miss C's reference to the screen, through which she had only caught glimpses of the others enjoying themselves, would seem to link up with her reference to "closed doors" at home, with the implication of secrecy and guilt about her own and her parents' activities and her fear of punishment.

The whole incident seemed to illustrate the submissive and self-punishing attitude that appeared to have characterized her throughout life.

SEQUEL

Some months later the almoner received a letter from Miss C saying that she had revisited the hospital during the almoner's holiday.

Miss C said that she had "taken the doctor's advice" and retired from work, the firm had settled a small pension on her, her sister was paying her a small sum for keeping her rooms clean and tidy, and the sister and brother-in-law were paying two-thirds instead of one-half of the rent. "So", said Miss C, "I manage very well." She said that the four weeks at the convalescent home had been "just what I needed". She had never slept so well in her life and "everyone has been very kind".

From the way in which the family appeared to have risen to the occasion, it would seem that Miss C's anxiety about them had, indeed, been coloured by emotional attitudes carried over from childhood, and perhaps the almoner's main service to this patient had been to lessen her guilt sufficiently to enable her to come to some more or less satisfactory terms with the situation.

CHAPTER 8

Casework with a Probationer

This is the case of a young man of seventeen who was placed on probation for an offence of larceny in which he was jointly concerned with several other youths. It was evident from information available that John was only very casually involved. Limited contact with John was established before the Court appearance and, although it was possible to obtain some idea of the problems involved, it was not until later in the period of supervision that a more accurate impression of the difficulties emerged.

Although John was under supervision for two years in all, descriptive material applies particularly to the first year of probation. Interviews were arranged at the usual regular weekly intervals; after three months, when greater confidence in the diagnosis was felt, frequency of meeting was reduced to once every two weeks. However, these arrangements were not inelastic, and numerous adjustments were made to meet the demands of John's studies and various crises that called for the immediate attention of the probation officer. Whenever it was necessary for the probation officer to break an appointment, it was made clear to John that the situation was completely unavoidable.

During the first year there were thirty-three individual interviews of approximately thirty minutes duration, and eight visits to the home. The illustrative interviews that follow were the first, fourteenth, and thirtieth.

John was a tall, dark, willowy young man, who chose to wear his hair long and adopt a rather casual form of dress. His manner seemed vague and preoccupied, and when addressing other people he would stand awkwardly holding his head to one side, creating an appearance of apology and self-effacement. He was the youngest of five children, having a married brother and sister living away from home and another brother and sister still single and living with the parents. The home was very modest, of the standard one would expect to find in a small urban, working-class community in the north of England.

Mr. B was in regular employment as an unskilled labourer and the older brothers and sisters were employed in various semi-skilled capacities. John was obviously the outstanding exception, having shown evidence of superior intelligence from an early age and been successful in the scholarship examination when eleven years old. Until his Court appearance he had been attending a local grammar school and, in spite of indications that he had not been working anywhere near his true capacity, he had not been unsuccessful. Although none of the immediate family had received advanced education, some brothers and sisters of both Mr. and Mrs. B had progressed in teaching and nursing careers.

During the initial enquiries little information was obtained about John's early history but even so there was no obviously abnormal psychopathology apart from some suggestion that his special position in the home had brought about subtle pressures in the form of parental expectations of academic and social success. This was underlined very clearly by the fact that in an area where higher education was not regarded as being particularly attractive and in spite of marked financial difficulty, the parents had done everything possible to keep the boy in his school and to meet the additional expenditure involved.

A few days after the Court hearing the probation officer called at the home to explain the nature of probation in general terms to the boy and his parents, and also to make appointments for interview in accordance with the requirements of the probation order. Much of the interview was concerned with the anxiety and guilt of the mother, which showed themselves in repeated utterances to the effect that "nothing like this has ever happened in my family before", and that as a result of this she had been "made very ill". The specific nature of her illness was never defined, but the theme of her remarks was to disclaim any responsibility for her son's behaviour, and to draw attention to the respectability not only of the immediate family but also of her own and her husband's parents. It was only after the probation officer had acknowledged her difficulties, and had shown that this role was not to criticize but to try to understand the situation, that she was able to move on from the comparative security offered by her reactive symptoms to a discussion about the practical implications of supervision.

John was the only other person present during this interview, but he had very little to say for himself, although he was obviously paying very keen attention to the conversation. During most of this short visit, John walked around the room, often posing and affecting a great air of unconcern, which was belied by a pale, drawn face and anxious studied movements. It was further noticed that often when his mother made some slight grammatical error, he would smile to himself in a rather superior way and covertly glance sideways

111

to observe the probation officer's reaction. In fact, John displayed uneasiness not only in relation to this aspect of his mother's behaviour but also, for example, when the offer of a dilapidated, garment-littered chair, or tea in a damaged cup, drew attention to material inadequacies in the home.

The visit concluded after arrangements had been made for John to call to see the probation officer at his office on the following day, and the appointment had been accepted in an extremely off-hand manner.

INTERVIEW I

John came late to the office and again made virtually no advances in the initial phases of the interview; again his reaction was one of studied unconcern. It was necessary on this occasion to explain fully the terms and conditions of the probation order, since explanation had been limited on the previous day by an attempt to avoid over-complicating an already difficult situation. The formal wording of the conditions appeared to increase John's anxiety, and his subsequent remarks suggested further his attempts to dissociate himself from the situation. He spoke of how "some people" had "problems and criminal tendencies", and then proceeded to emphasize how he could not in any way be included in this class, because there was "nothing wrong with *me*". Moreover, he had "not committed my offence with any idea of gain", and in fact had only behaved as he did out of a "sense of obligation" to the other youths concerned with him. He added that he could "understand that it is the probation officer's job to look for problems" and that he could see that "some people would need help to put them on the right path". He thus suggested that, although probation might be all very well for some people, there was certainly no need for action as far as he was concerned. At this point the probation officer said that the present situation must be very

112

difficult for John if he believed that he was to be treated as a "delinquent" being scrutinized for "bad" or "abnormal" qualities. John smiled wanly, and responded by arguing that "everyone" thought this way as it was "only natural" for people to believe that he had "criminal inferiority". He described the reaction of his parents, neighbours, and teachers to the news of his conduct. Eventually the probation officer said he supposed it was not surprising that John could not anticipate any different treatment and so had to adopt a keep-off attitude; John then relaxed slightly and commenced talking about some of his immediate difficulties.

John was anxious to continue his studies and the remainder of the interview was devoted to discussing the availability of courses and application procedure. However, just before leaving the office, he returned to the subject of probation. "Will my home be visited again?" And, "When will my next appointment be, as I don't come into town very often?" These remarks were again interpreted as indications of inability to accept the situation, and while no attempt was made to ignore the legal obligations that the Order placed on John, acknowledgment of his difficulty was repeated. Moreover, some of his very evident concern about contact with his home seemed to spring from an idea that interviews were not completely confidential, and reassurance on this point did not appear to give him much satisfaction.

During the next few weeks it was necessary to handle John's evident reluctance to keep appointments, and the interviews carried out during these rather erratic attendances were characterized by the kind of remark that had emerged during the first interview. On one occasion, for example, he said, "I have not been to lectures in town this week and I saw no reason to come", and expressed once again his conviction that he was to be "put in the right way of life" because of his delinquent motives. However, it was noticed that as time went on he showed an increasing unwillingness to leave the office at the end of an interview, began to come on time, and although his conversation was at times very confused and composed of long, wordy, and apparently meaningless phrases, he commenced making oblique references to his feelings and problems encountered at home. It was not always possible to perceive the full significance of his remarks, but occasionally John's emotional attitude as he talked gave the probation officer some more definite pointer on which to base his remarks. This was illustrated very clearly when John opened one interview by referring to a television documentary about a school for disturbed boys. John had been greatly impressed by the understanding shown by the headmaster when faced by provocative and ambivalent behaviour on the part of one boy who had, according to John, "had an unhappy family life".

The graphic and sensitive manner in which the play was described suggested that the situation had been a singularly meaningful one for John. The probation officer therefore suggested that perhaps he had noticed some similarities in the probation relationship, and would welcome the type of understanding and help displayed by the headmaster in the documentary. In the subsequent discussion John admitted that at first he had believed the probation officer's main concern would be the negative one of "checking up on me all the time", but now he was "beginning to see that this is not the case". However, although John's own views were beginning to change, he complained that, as in so many other things, those of his parents were not so readily modified. They, he said, were always ready to use the probation officer as a threat, and he was irritated to see that even after he had tried to explain they still could not understand that "this is different". However, even this apparently minor criticism of his parents was followed by extensive justification for their

114

behaviour; discussion around this helped him to admit that he found it imperative to prevent the probation officer from thinking "unpleasant" things about him, which he was "sure are seen" and "hoped for". He also disclosed that he had thought the root of probation was "probe", and that this described the probation officer's function.

Comment
(a) In probation, unlike many other forms of social casework, it is necessary for both the client and social worker to operate within a clearly defined legal framework, which often involves the additional handicap of dealing with a client who has not willingly asked for help. Penalties for non-compliance with an Order can be severe, and in this case it was necessary for the probation officer to handle John's passively negative behaviour with great care and to anticipate some acting out in the form of failure to keep appointments. In the early stages of supervision John was completely incapable of accepting that in probation he would encounter a form of relationship that was an improvement on past experiences, and the probation officer therefore made no attempt to state his good intentions. Indeed, with John's harsh preconceptions and statements to the effect that there was nothing wrong with *him*, such action could only have increased antagonism. Instead, the officer tried to reach the limited immediate objective of showing that, legal considerations apart, he would *try* to understand John and the difficulties he faced. That John could expect something different was therefore deliberately implied from the first interview onwards.

For example, when the probation officer said that the situation must be difficult if John believed he was to be treated as a delinquent being scrutinized for bad or abnormal qualities, John was able to see that his own feelings were being considered. It was felt that this had greater significance for the boy than if the probation officer had merely said that John's fears were groundless. Later, when the probation officer said it was not surprising that John could not anticipate any different treatment, he was again showing his attempt to put himself in the boy's place and suggesting that, although his parents and other people had condemned, he would not.

Subsequently every opportunity was sought to draw attention to the positive features in John's behaviour, such as his reluctance to terminate an interview, and eventually John was enabled to overcome his rigid denial that he had any problems at all. Admittedly, he could not at this point openly allow a personal need, but he could nevertheless accept, without undue anxiety, suggestions by the probation officer that the television programme had a special significance for him and that the description represented a means of communication. On this occasion, as on many others in the future, John showed a tendency to talk in objective terms about incidents and situations that in many respects were parallel to the probation situation.

(b) Although background information was scant, the precarious nature of John's personal relationships was suggested by his reactions in the interview and at home, his motivation in the offence, and a school record that commented upon his need to "dramatize" himself. Combined with these factors were the normal conflict of adolescence, and stresses usually associated with educationally-induced class mobility.

In view of all these circumstances, it was necessary for the probation officer to make some decision as to where he would focus attention. The deciding factor proved to be John's age, and the fact that his dependency on the home was not nearly so great as it would have been in a younger child. Ideally, of course, contact should be continuous with all members of the family under such circumstances, but in this case, as in so many others, it was necessary for the probation officer to make the most of a limited time at his disposal.

(c) John's anxiety about visits to his home, as shown at the end of the first interview, was not particularly unusual. Very often at the beginning of supervision the probation officer has to assure the probationer that what he says will be kept confidential and will not be reported even to his parents without his express knowledge and permission. In a situation such as probation, where one person has contact with several members of a family, this approach is absolutely essential if a position of trust is to be established and maintained. The assurances given to John were also given at a later stage to both parents. It seemed evident that John was afraid that any expression of disloyalty or hostility on his part might be disclosed to his parents at some time, and purely verbal reassurances on this point did little to help him at first. It took time for him to realize that his confidences and those of his parents were respected; he then felt able to talk more freely about himself.

The following interview occurred during the period when the relationship was beginning to develop, and is typical of a number of interviews that took place during the fourth and fifth month.

INTERVIEW II

The probation officer was surprised to see John at the office; it was the day before his appointment, it was earlier than usual, and on a morning when John had to sit an examination. He seemed sheepish and ill at ease and obviously found difficulty in opening up the conversation, so the probation officer mentioned the examination and the chance John had taken of calling at a time when he was not normally available.

I   117

The boy replied resignedly that he expected there were a lot of other important things the probation officer had to do, but that as he happened to be "passing by" the office he had decided to call in before instead of after his examination. The probation officer suggested that perhaps he was feeling unsettled and needed a sense of support; he agreed, adding that this was not easy for him to obtain. Given some encouragement, he went on to say that there were some things he could not talk about at home, particularly ideas of failure, because "they are not the sort of people who would understand". He said this reminded him of something he had wanted to show the probation officer, and pulled from his pocket an extract from a book, which he said was appropriate to the talks they had been having and which more ably described his feelings. Condensed, this article referred to "aimless people" who had nothing to look forward to and who were "casually haphazard and without plan or purpose". It described how a man known to the author punctuated his day with what the more active would regard as mere trifles. On a railway journey he would look forward to his lunch with "his desires and appetites mounting as the hour approached". At home, the man would look forward to going out to buy an evening paper and to sitting back for an hour reading it. The article went on, "That presents the picture in its simplest form, and from a man of his years we could hardly expect much more—we who are younger and more active *need* a plan and a purpose." The word need had been underlined.

Having read the article the probation officer drew attention to the underlining and, when this caused John to colour up, went on to suggest that by bringing the article John had shown that he had been thinking about the kind of thing they had been discussing and wished to draw attention to this fact. The probation officer said that looking at it in this way he could understand John's only partial resignation when he observed that there were demands of other clients to be met. John admitted that he had wondered how much interest would be shown in him, was convinced that his contribution was greatest, and knew that this couldn't be otherwise. His views on allocation of the probation officer's time were not disputed, but instead attention was drawn to John's wishes for *at least* a relationship of equally balanced interest and his dissatisfaction with the present situation in spite of a realistic evaluation. After some thought John smiled, but then remarked that in a way he had "expected something different", because "Councils are not interested in people, only numbers and names on papers". He then revealed that his expectation of authority was always the same, that people would be uninterested or prejudiced. He could not, therefore, experience any sense of obligation to them and felt justified in taking advantage of bodies such as the Education Department, which were without personality and individual interest. In Court, for example, "I knew I should have felt ashamed", and had acted that way because it was expected of him, but in fact he was much more concerned with the behaviour of people holding responsible, authoritative positions who were saying untrue things about him. John had some difficulty in describing his feelings but ultimately, and very reluctantly, admitted his contempt.

The probation officer concluded by asking John if he had noticed how the complaints about Councils and Courts resembled the remarks he made about his family's behaviour. John said, "I suppose the feeling is the same," but could not accept a subsequent suggestion that he had expected lack of interest and prejudice from the probation officer and had behaved towards him accordingly. Reminders of past incidents could not move him from the view that "this is different—you are trying to help".

During the next few months John showed an increasing readiness to call into the office and talk about immediate difficulties, often in the guise of practical problems he was encountering in his studies. It was possible to give him some practical help about these, but even this had direct and immediate repercussions as far as the probation relationship was concerned. For example, an interview immediately following an occasion when he had been loaned some textbooks was concerned with a play he had seen. This was about an ambitious young artisan who felt himself unable to make a success in industry until he had obtained ideas and equipment from another person and used these to his own advantage. Once successful, his improved financial standing permitted a greater degree of class mobility,and created difficulties in a marriage to a woman of "higher class". The underlying significance of this was not overlooked and the probation officer related it both to John's relationship with him and to the problems John encountered in his attempts at adjustment.

During this period John contacted other people in authoritative positions three times and was agreeably surprised by the attention he received from them.

Visits to John's home were regular but not frequent, and on nearly every occasion it was necessary to concentrate on the poor communication between the parents and their son. John's picture of his home was exaggerated, but the parents nevertheless appeared rigid and unimaginative, and it was some time before they could appreciate that John's failure to take them completely into his confidence was not a complete rejection of them as parents It was clear that John had been identified with the more successful of the parental siblings and this appeared to produce feelings of inferiority and resentment in their relationship with the boy. Eventually the parents became better able to understand the role of the probation officer and were not so ready to use him as a threat.

120

Comment

(a) John had now reached a point in treatment where he openly demonstrated that the probation relationship had significance for him, but in making this admission he needed reassurance that the relationship would not be one-sided. His capacity for realistic assessment of the situation did little to reduce a fundamental wish for the unlimited understanding and gratification that he implied had been denied him in his primary relationships. Furthermore, the increased frequency of his visits strongly suggested an attempt to assess the extent of the probation officer's interest and his capacity to meet his demands. That John doubted this capacity in the probation officer, and in fact in anyone in "authority", implied that the demands were likely to be excessive, and here the contents of the article and John's reaction to help were illuminating.

(b) There appeared little doubt that John's fantasies about the behaviour of authority figures contained residues of past experiences, both actual and as *perceived* by him. However, through his relationship with the probation officer he now had to admit that there were discrepancies between these views and reality and inevitably this began to create difficulties for him. Hitherto, the hostility and resentment produced by a feeling of deprivation were not directed at specific personalities, but at depersonalized bodies that could be taken advantage of without *personal* involvement. In Court, for example, he did not *feel* ashamed, but he could adopt a detached and contemptuous standpoint merely by registering the emotions he believed other people expected him to experience. In essence, therefore, John's problems appeared to display two principal features. First, if the probation officer was not the type of person he was expected to be, then it meant that John had been acting with unjustified hostility and this implied personal responsibility for "unpleasant" thoughts and behaviour. Moreover, if this were so in the relationship with the probation officer, then it could equally be so in the relationships within his family. Second, John would have to tolerate the discomfort of this realization and decide whether he could bear to reveal this facet of himself to the probation officer or whether it would be safer to act a part by anticipating his reactions.

INTERVIEW III

John now seemed much more secure in the interview and was able to remove his top-coat and select the chair he always chose to use. In response to a general enquiry about how he was getting on, he said in a very provocative fashion that things were going "as well as can be expected with my limited ability". With earlier discussions in mind, the probation officer observed that it often seemed necessary for him to make derogatory remarks about his ability and attainments, even when they both knew that this was not necessary. Perhaps he really believed he had ability, but he did not like to admit this openly in case he might be attacked as being "uppish". He paused at this and then in a spuriously off-handed manner said, "It happens like that at home sometimes", and went on to explain that he usually spent a substantial part of the evening studying in his room, joining the rest of the family later to watch T.V. Often the rest of the family would accuse him of dodging household duties and thinking himself too good for them. This was unfair, he thought, because even when looking in he would not consciously ignore the rest of the family, but would be preoccupied with thoughts about his work. The probation officer said he seemed to feel that the others were jealous of his different interests, aims, and abilities, and because this at times made him feel guilty he would play himself down rather than experience anxiety about a lot of "bad feeling".

122

The probation officer then suggested that he might also do this to people outside the home, including the probation officer. He looked up at this point and said, "That's right, exactly right", but immediately showed some signs of embarrassment and, pausing, said, "I do not want to paint too drastic a picture, because in many ways we get on together quite well at home."

There followed a great deal of justification for the attitude of his parents, brother, and sister, in which he was clearly showing his ability to make allowances for them. The probation officer suggested that in spite of these excuses for his family he did feel annoyed with them for adopting this attitude; John agreed, but said the problem did not often arise because he could "split off" his family from his other activities. In a sense he thought that he could live equally comfortably in "dirt or Rolls Royce". The probation officer remarked that this was not the first time John had shown a tendency to think in extremes, and wondered if John's solution was as effective as he suggested. They had noticed, for example, that he was unsure of people's responses and could not rid himself of the feeling that he was different from other people even when he was well removed from his home. John partly acknowledged this, adding, "Of course, some people have not got the disadvantage of having a background of inferiority." Asked what he meant by this, he said, "Other people are not subjected to a lot of shouting when things go wrong." He said that recently some friends of the family had come to the house bringing their three-year-old daughter, and while the rest of the family had their meal at the table, the child was allowed to sit in front of the fire. During the meal she spilt her food on the carpet, all the family then started shouting at her and she did not know what to do. The probation officer thought John was easily able to put himself in the child's place; he vigorously agreed, saying that he knew how she felt in this situation, as he himself had been similarly treated. The effect was to make him feel "dazed".

The probation officer thought John felt that continuous treatment of this type made him uncertain how to react not only towards his own parents but towards other people. It was also suggested that he felt this background put him at a disadvantage with those whose background was more fortunate.

The probation officer and John had already noticed John's uncertainty in reacting to other people and his anxiety in case he should produce hostile reactions. John responded bitterly that "the poor are always on the defensive".

At this point he produced some cigarettes, and was obviously very anxious when the probation officer chose to smoke his own inferior brand. The officer felt he must have failed to conform to John's expectation of him and remarked on John's apparent concern. John responded that he would "be much happier" if the probation officer had one of his cigarettes, and later said, "It does not seem right for you to smoke that sort of cigarette." The probation officer suggested that this was an example of the sort of thing they had just been talking about; that John had definite ideas about the things the probation officer should do and have, which did not include smoking cheap cigarettes. John agreed, and nodded at the further suggestion that it was another example of the unfounded expectation that other people would have much more than he had. Because the probation officer's behaviour had not fitted in with his scheme of thinking, John became very "confused".

The concluding discussion centred around his need to keep his life in separate compartments, with particular attention to the fact that it was only when he brought them together and saw his home in relation to other groups of people that he felt angry. This produced a very marked response and he denied that he *ever* felt angry. The probation officer doubted this and suggested that he did not like to admit having very strong feelings of this type. He then said smilingly, "I suppose I do have these feelings at times", and quoted one example of difficulties at school when he had hated his head teacher. This had not been easy for him latterly, because during recent contact he had found this head teacher to be a most helpful and understanding person. The probation officer thought it was always difficult to find that people he had hated could also have a lot of good in them, and wondered if this was the sort of difficulty he often encountered at home, since they had also noticed this in his relationship with the probation officer (e.g. his strong denial of annoyance at absences on leave, and a feeling that the probation officer had things that John had not). John thought quite a long time about this, and eventually said, "Yes, that feels right, but I am rather confused." The probation officer wondered if perhaps he was distressed at being made to feel this way, to which he replied, "No, not at all. Often you have made me feel like this but I go away and think about it and it has helped me."

Comment

(a) This interview took place at the end of a year of supervision and in many ways represented a marked contrast to those previously recorded. Not only did John's behaviour imply a knowledge that he would be able to make himself comfortable and be assured of a measure of individual attention, but he was also able to make the type of remark that he knew would be taken up by the probation officer. This was attributable to the fact that, having been helped to verbalize some of the more negative aspects of his emotional relationships with others, he found with relief that admissions on his part in no way affected his relationship with the probation officer, who was equally prepared to see his positive qualities.

(b) John's unprompted description of his method of coping with difficult emotions and situations, by "splitting off" his life into separate compartments, appeared to be completely in character with his whole behaviour-pattern and gave some indication of the stresses under which he laboured. In reality, of course, this way of handling situations was bound to have repercussions in his home life and his contacts with other people, and to make heavy demands on his mental energies.

In order, therefore, to help John it was necessary to show him in the relationship that he could experience positive and negative emotions towards the probation officer, and that these were not the product of a "down to earth" evaluation but of *perception* coloured by past affective experiences. Once John could see this in relation to the probation officer, he could then carry these experiences into other relationships, as occurred with his head teacher, whom he had originally condemned out of hand. The "confusion" that accompanied this realization appeared to be produced by relinquishing his habitual denial of such powerful emotions as anger and consciously admitting that he had been angry with those for whom he had affection and that he found good qualities in those he had previously regarded as condemning and prejudiced. It was not surprising that hitherto John had found difficulty in relating to other people, since he had projected on to them the very emotions and attitudes he denied in himself, and had therefore to "dramatize" himself and act the particular role that he imagined was demanded by a situation.

CONCLUSION

It has not been possible to give a comprehensive picture of John's total behaviour-pattern or of all aspects of treatment. Emphasis has been given to those difficulties that seemed by the probation officer to be most pressing and most obviously connected with the delinquency.

Obviously John's superior intelligence facilitated communication and progress. In the limited time available, the techniques employed were not essentially different from those normally used by the probation officer. Although intellectual considerations must not be overlooked, their importance is reduced in an approach of this type, where considerable attention is paid to the *emotional* significance of the relationship. What appeared to be most meaningful to John was the fact that he was encouraged to discuss his difficulties with the probation officer on the basis that at the outset neither of them knew the answers to problems, but would jointly look for an understanding and a solution. In fact John was, at a later stage, able to refer to "our mutual problem".

As later events showed, John increasingly became able to make a natural approach to other people, and in the words of one teacher who had known him for several years "he seemed much more sensible". It also appeared that the lessening preoccupation with fantasy situations enabled him to utilize his mental energies more economically, with the result that he worked better and showed increasing academic promise.

127

BIBLIOGRAPHY

ASSOCIATION OF PSYCHIATRIC SOCIAL WORKERS (1956). *Boundaries of case work*. London.

BIESTEK, F. (1961). *The casework relationship*. London: George Allen & Unwin.

BOWLBY, J. (1951). *Maternal care and mental health*. Geneva: W.H.O.; London: H.M.S.O.; New York: Columbia University Press. Abridged version *Child care and the growth of love*. Harmondsworth: Pelican Books A271, 1953.

BRITTON, CLARE. (1955). Casework techniques in the child care service. *Case Conference* 1, No. 9, January.

ELKAN, I. (1953). Psychiatric social work in a children's reception centre. *Brit. J. psychiat. soc. Wk* No. 8, November.

ELKAN, I. (1956). Interviews with neglectful parents. *Brit. J. psychiat. soc. Wk* 3, No. 3.

ELLES, G. W. (1961). Collateral treatment in a family by psycho-analytic techniques. *Brit. J. psychiat. soc. Wk* 6, No. 1.

FAMILY DISCUSSION BUREAU (1955). *Social casework in marital problems*. London: Tavistock Publications.

FAMILY DISCUSSION BUREAU (1960). *Marriage: Studies in emotional conflict and growth*. London: Methuen.

FLÜGEL, J. C. (1929). *Psychoanalytic study of the family*. London: Hogarth Press.

FREUD, S. (1924). *Collected Papers*. Vols. I-V. London: Hogarth Press.

GOLDBERG, E. M. (1953). The function and use of relationship in psychiatric social work. *Brit. J. psychiat. soc. Wk* No. 8, November.

HUNNYBUN, NOËL K. (1955). The use of the relationship in casework with parents. In the *Report of XI Interclinic Conference for staffs of Child Guidance Clinics*. London: National Association for Mental Health.

IRVINE, E. E. (1954). Research into problem families. *Brit. J. psychiat. soc. Wk* **9.**

IRVINE, E. E. (1956). Transference and reality in the casework relationship. *Brit. J. psychiat. soc. Wk* 3, No. 4.

KLEIN, MELANIE & RIVIERE, JOAN (1953). *Love, hate, and reparation.* Psycho-analytical Epitomes No. 2. London: Hogarth Press.

MASON, E. M. (1956). The centenary of Freud: understandings and misunderstandings. *Brit. J. psychiat. soc. Wk* 3, No. 4.

MODEL, A. (1957). Psychotherapy in general practice: opportunities and limitations. *Brit. J. psychiat. soc. Wk* **4,** No. 1.

PERLMAN, HELEN H. (1957). *Social casework: a problem-solving process.* University of Chicago Press; Cambridge University Press.

SHARPE, ELLA F. (1950). *Collected papers on psychoanalysis.* London: Hogarth Press.

STRACHEY, J. (1934). The nature of the therapeutic action of psycho-analysis. *Int. J. Psycho-Anal.*

INDEX

advice,
    failure to follow, 51
    limitations of, 50 ff.
agency, client's image of, 35
ambivalence, of feeling, 15
approach, client's, reasons for, 39, 51, 57, 87
approval, desire for, 53
attitudes, maternal, 16, 23-5
authority, and conscience, 21

Brown, Ivor, 14 f.

cases (in order of discussion)
    woman, seeking financial aid, 6 f.
    woman, uncertain whether to relinquish job, 9
    woman, seeking housing help, subsequently disclosing marital problem, 12
    woman, illustrating transference of feelings from past on to caseworker, 31
    woman, illustrating unconscious desire to be thought of as a child, 37
    woman, illustrating importance of client's opening remark, 43 f.

    man, illustrating use of advice so as to ensure its failure, 51
    woman, illustrating possible danger of yielding to request for advice, 52 f.
    parents, illustrating danger of involvement of caseworker's personal feelings, 54 f.
    woman, illustrating use of opportunity to work out client's affectional needs, 56
    woman, illustrating usefulness of client's "thinking aloud", 59
    man, illustrating use of interview for ego-strengthening, 61 f.
    woman, illustrating revelation of transferences of feeling, 68 ff.
    woman, illustrating value of opportunity to experience warm feelings towards caseworker, 72 f.
    woman, illustrating associative linking of present with past experiences, 75 f.

131

132

mother, good and bad, 18 f.

Oedipus complex, 20
office, arrangement of, 36
opening remarks, importance
of, 43 f.
over-valuation of caseworker,
74

perceptiveness, intuitive, 33
power, caseworker's desire for,
57
probation, 109 ff.
projection, 45, 88
of child's feelings on to
mother, 18
psycho-analysis,
object of, 29
value of, 4 f., 13

qualities, personal, of caseworker, 48 ff.
questions,
framing of, 38 f.
"open-ended", 39, 88

reassurance, limitations of, 49 f.
reception, client's reaction to,
36

regression, in psycho-analysis,
75
repression, and guilt, 22
rigidity, 21 f.

security, child's, and mother, 19
self-awareness, 34-5
child's, 17
sublimation, 21
suckling, 17
super-ego, 63
see also conscience
supportive work, 60 ff.

tension, overcoming, 68 f.
"thinking aloud", 58
transference, 28 ff.
in casework, 30
example of, 31
positive, 71 ff.
use of, 67 ff.
triangular situations, 20

unconscious,
behaviour, understanding of,
43
influence of, 5
interpretation of, 29
part played by, 5 ff.